Contents

1 Venus of Lespugue. Aurignacian period, France. Distorted female fertility figure showing loin-cloth formed of twisted strands of wool or flax

A Concise History of Costume

A Concise History of
Costume

James Laver

314 illustrations, 58 in colour

Thames and Hudson · London

TO MRS DORIS LANGLEY MOORE
COLLECTOR, AUTHOR, FRIEND

391.009 LAV

PRINTED IN GREAT BRITAIN BY JARROLD AND SONS LTD, NORWICH

ISBN 0 500 18092 X CLOTHBOUND
ISBN 0 500 20084 X PAPERBACK

CHAPTER ONE

How it all began

COSTUME, throughout the greater part of its history, has followed two separate lines of development, resulting in two contrasting types of garment. The most obvious line of division in modern eyes is between male and female dress: trousers and skirts. But it is by no means true that men have always worn bifurcated clothes and women not. The Greeks and Romans wore tunics, that is to say, skirts. Mountain people like the Scots and the modern Greeks wear what are, in effect, skirts. Far Eastern and Near Eastern women have worn trousers, and many continue to do so. The sex division turns out not to be a true division at all.

It is possible to contrast 'fitted' and 'draped' clothes, most modern clothes falling into the first category and Ancient Greek clothes, for example, into the other. History has shown many variations in this respect, and it is possible to find intermediate types. Perhaps the most useful distinction is that drawn by the anthropologists between 'tropical' and 'arctic' dress.

The great ancient civilizations arose in the fertile valleys of the Euphrates, the Nile and the Indus: all tropical areas, where protection from the cold cannot have been the dominant motive for wearing clothes. Many such motives have been adduced, ranging from the naïve idea, based on the story in Genesis, that clothes were worn for reasons of modesty, to the sophisticated notion that they were worn for reasons of display and protective magic. The psychology of clothes, however, has been adequately dealt with elsewhere. In the present study it is proposed largely to ignore these complications and to concentrate on the two questions of form and material.

2, 3 A seated
woman and a
king from
Mari. Sumerian,
c. 2900–2685 BC.
Skirt and shawl
are built up of
twisted tufts of
wool or flax
arranged in
flounces

The early civilizations of Egypt and Mesopotamia are far
from being the whole story. Within recent years a much more
primitive documentation has become available, largely owing
to the discovery and study of cave paintings. Geologists have
made us aware of a succession of Ice Ages when the climate of
a large part of Europe was extremely cold. Even in the last of
the Palaeolithic cultures (that is, cultures in which tools and
weapons were made by chipping hard stones like flints) life
was lived, as it were, on the edge of the great glaciers which
covered much of the continent. In such circumstances, although
details of clothing may have been determined by social and
psychological considerations, the main motive in covering the
body was to keep out the cold, since nature had proved so
niggardly in providing *homo sapiens* with a natural coat of fur.

The animals were more fortunate, and primitive man soon
realized that they could be hunted and killed not only for their

4 The god Abu(?) and a female statue from Tell Asmar. Sumerian, early
third millennium BC. The loin-cloth has become recognizably a skirt and
the twisted tufts have shrunk to a fringe

flesh but for their pelts. In other words he began to wear furs. This presented him with two problems. Not only was the skin of a beast merely wrapped round the shoulders very hampering to his movements, but it left part of the body exposed. He therefore desired to *shape* it in some way, even if at first he had no means of doing so.

The second problem is that the skins of animals, as they dry, become very hard and intractable. Some method had to be found of making them soft and pliable; the simplest method of doing this is by a laborious mastication. Eskimo women to the present day spend a considerable part of their time *chewing* the hides which their husbands bring home from the chase. Another method consists of alternately wetting the hide and beating it with a mallet, having first scraped off any fragments of flesh which may still be adhering to it. Neither process is very satisfactory, however, for, if the hides become wet, the whole labour has to be repeated.

An advance was made when it was discovered that oil or blubber rubbed into the skin helped to keep it pliable for a longer time, that is, until the oil dried out. The next step was the discovery of tanning, and it is strange to think that the essential techniques of this process, so primitive in their inception, are still in use today. The bark of certain trees, notably the oak and the willow, contains tannic acid which can be extracted by soaking the bark in water. The hides are then immersed for considerable periods in the solution and emerge from this process permanently pliable and waterproof.

Such prepared pelts could also be cut and shaped, and we now come to one of the greatest technological advances in human history, comparable in importance to the invention of the wheel and the discovery of fire: the invention of the eyed needle. Large numbers of such needles, made of mammoth ivory, the bones of the reindeer and the tusks of the walrus, have been found in Palaeolithic caves, where they were deposited forty thousand years ago. Some of them are quite small and of exquisite workmanship. This invention made it possible to sew pieces of hide together to make them fit the body. The result was the kind of clothing still worn by the Eskimo.

Meanwhile, people living in somewhat more temperate climates were discovering the use of animal and vegetable fibres. It is probable that felting was the first step. In this process, developed in Central Asia by the ancestors of the Mongols, wool or hair is combed out, wetted and placed in layers on a mat. The mat is then rolled up tightly and beaten with a stick. The strands of hair or wool are thus matted together and the felt produced is warm, pliable and durable and can be cut and sewn to make garments, rugs and tents.

Another primitive method, also using vegetable fibres, was to make use of the bark of certain trees such as the mulberry or fig. The bark was stripped off and soaked in water. Three layers were then placed on a flat stone, the grain of the middle layer being at right angles to the other two. The layers were then beaten with a mallet until they clung together and the bark cloth resulting was oiled or painted to add to its durability. This process, very similar to that used by the Ancient Egyptians to convert papyrus into a writing material, might be regarded as a half-way house between matting and weaving. Bark cloth, however, is not easily cut or sewn, and garments made of it are usually draperies made from a single rectangle of material.

Bark fibres can be used for true weaving, as was done by some American Indians, but they are not as satisfactory as other vegetable fibres such as flax, hemp and cotton. These, however, require cultivation and are therefore little used by nomadic people in the pastoral stage. Such people had sheep, and wool seems to have been employed in the Neolithic period. In the New World the useful animals were the llama, the alpaca and the vicuña.

Weaving on any extensive scale requires a fixed abode, since a loom tends to be large and heavy and therefore difficult to transport from place to place. The ideal situation for development was a small, settled community surrounded by grazing lands for sheep. The fleece was clipped off by methods closely

5 Assurbanipal II from Nimrud. Babylonian, 883–859 BC. Male costume consisting of a long tunic with close-fitting sleeves. The diagonal fringes of the skirt are formed by a shawl thrown over one shoulder

6 Persian tribute-bearer from Persepolis, fifth century BC. The feet are booted, and the headdress is formed of a band of material

resembling those in use today; the resultant bunch of fibre was then spun off and the thread woven into cloth on a loom. Once cloth manufacture, on however small a scale, had been established, the way was open for the development of costume as we know it.

The simplest method of using cloth for what is significantly termed 'clothing' was to wrap a small rectangle of it round the waist, thus making a sarong, the primitive form of the skirt. Later, another square of cloth was draped over the

7 Persian archers from Susa, fifth–fourth century B C. Tunics made of patterned material, belted and with wide sleeves. The hair and beards were curled by means of hot tongs

shoulders and kept in place by fibulae. Clothing of this nature was used by the Egyptians, the Assyrians, the Greeks and the Romans. In fact draped clothes were the mark of civilization. Tailored clothes were regarded as 'barbarian' and the Romans at one time went so far as to decree the death penalty for wearing them.

Draped clothes plainly required a considerable development in the art of weaving in order to produce rectangles of cloth large enough for the purpose. The transition from skins of beasts to woven cloth was not, however, as simple or as immediate as was once supposed. Statuettes and bas-reliefs of the ancient Sumerian civilization of Mesopotamia (third millennium B C) show figures wearing skirts composed of tufted

Ills. 2–4 tissues: that is, cloth which presents the appearance of tufts of wool arranged symmetrically, sometimes as a series of flounces. Once the tufts, or independent strands, were relegated to the borders of the cloth rectangles, they became a fringe, and this vestigial element can be seen very plainly in almost all the garments worn by Assyrians and Babylonians of both sexes.

It has been pointed out that the fringed shawls (for that would seem the most rewarding way to think of them) com-

Ill. 5 posing the costume of, for example, Assurbanipal, as seen in his statue in the British Museum, are shown much more tightly draped about the body than could have been the case in real life. The sculptor has eliminated all folds and wrinkles in order to portray more clearly the patterns of the figured cloth.

Women and high dignitaries continued to wear garments of this kind, but they were gradually replaced in ordinary male costume by a kind of tunic with sleeves. It is thought that the sleeves were due to the influence of the mountain people round about, as were also the closed boots. Both would seem to have been unnecessary in the very hot climate of the Euphrates and the Tigris valleys.

Women are seldom represented in the bas-reliefs found at Nineveh, although they are rich in representations of male costume. There are, however, certain statues of goddesses

14

which show them in long, flounced robes. It is interesting to note that an Assyrian law of about 1200 BC compelled married women to wear veils in public, the earliest record of a custom which has prevailed in these districts until modern times. The hair was worn long by both sexes. Hair and beards were curled and sometimes interwoven with gold thread. Men's headgear was in the shape of an inverted flower-pot, although warriors, of course, wore helmets, terminating in a kind of blunt spike. Protective clothing was at first of leather, later covered, for the heavy infantry and cavalry, with metal plaques.

The Persians overran the Babylonian civilization in the sixth century BC. Since they came from the colder climate of the mountains of what is now called Turkistan, they wore warmer clothes but soon abandoned these for the fringed tunics and overmantles of the conquered race. In addition to wool and linen they now had access to silk, brought from China by the long caravan route. They retained, however, their character- istic headdress, the soft felt cap which the Greeks called 'Phrygian' and which, some two thousand years later, was adopted by the French revolutionaries as 'the red cap of Liberty'. They also kept their characteristic footgear, a closed boot of supple leather slightly turned up at the toe. The most important innovation was the wearing of trousers, which came to be looked upon as the typical Persian garment and, if we can rely on the very scanty records available, were probably worn by women also.

Ill. 7

Ill. 6

The Medes who shared in the Persian conquests were of the same race and wore similar garments, but looser and more voluminous. The headdresses also were different, consisting either of a round cap with a flat crown or of a hood. There was little contrast in male and female costume except that the women's coats were wider and longer. But it would be profitless, within the limits of this brief survey, to attempt to establish minor differences in costume between Persians and Medes, and the still semi-nomadic people, such as the Scythians, the Dacians and the Sarmatians of the neighbouring steppes.

15

8 Banquet scene from a tomb in Thebes, XVIII Dynasty, 1555–1330 B C. The dancers wear bead girdles, which are plainly visible through the diaphanous material of the long tunic – an early example of the 'see-through' dress

The valley of the Nile is no hotter than the valley of the Euphrates, but Egyptian costume was much scantier and lighter than that of Assyria and Babylon. Indeed, many of the lower *Ill. 8* classes, and the slaves in the palaces, went about almost, if not completely, naked. The wearing of clothes was a kind of class distinction.

Fortunately, we know a great deal about Ancient Egyptian dress, from statuettes and wall-paintings, which, owing to the extremely dry climate, have been preserved in enormous numbers. The available documentation is greater than that of any other ancient civilization, and the most striking thing about it is its static quality. Over a period of nearly three thousand years the changes to be noted are minimal.

16

9 Tutankhamen and his queen, XVIII Dynasty, 1350–1340 B C. Royal costume differed from that of other Egyptians by being of finer material, with embroidered belts and collars of gold and enamel

During what is called the Old Kingdom (i.e. before 1500 BC)
the characteristic garment was the *schenti*, a piece of woven
material used as a loin-cloth and kept in place by a belt. For

Ill. 11 kings and dignitaries it was pleated and stiffened and sometimes embroidered. Under the New Kingdom (1500 BC to
332 BC) the Pharaohs also wore a long, fringed tunic called a
kalasiris, which, being semi-transparent, allowed the loin-cloth
to be seen underneath. It was made of a rectangular piece of
material and was sometimes woven in one piece, producing,
when worn by women, a tight-fitting garment finishing below
the breasts and kept in place by shoulder straps. (The extremely

Ill. 10 tight-fitting appearance of women's clothes in sculpture and
painting is probably due to the conventions of Egyptian art;
the actual garments were almost certainly more ample.) A
short cape sometimes covered the shoulders, or else the throat
was encircled with a wide, jewelled collar, leaving the breasts
exposed.

Unlike other ancient peoples the Egyptians made little use
of wool, since animal fibres were considered impure. After the
Alexandrian conquest, it came to be used in the fabrication of
ordinary garments but was still forbidden in the dress of priests
and in burial clothes. For these the finest linen was required.

The Ancient Egyptians had extremely high standards of
hygiene, and one of the advantages of fine linen garments was
that they could be easily washed. For similar reasons men
shaved their heads and wore a headdress made of a square of
striped material encircling the temples and forming square
pleats over the ears. On ceremonial occasions, wigs were worn,
sometimes made of natural hair, sometimes of flax or palm-
fibre. Such wigs have been found in early tombs, and the
custom of wearing them lasted for thousands of years.

The young princesses shown in frescoes also had shaven
heads, but mature women generally wore their own hair,
sometimes frizzed or waved. The Egyptians wore no hats.
What we see on the heads of the Pharaohs is a crown, or rather
two crowns, 'the crown of the North and the crown of the

10 Woman bearing offerings, XI–XII Dynasty, *c.* 2000 B C. The patterning on the tight-fitting dress is thought to have been composed of a coloured network of leather

11 King Akenaton and Queen Nefertite, XVIII Dynasty, 1555–1330 B C. The King wears the *schenti* or loin-cloth of fine pleated material, the Queen the long tunic, or *haik*, fastened at the waist. Both have deep collars of beads and jewels

South', one in the form of a circlet and the other in the form of a conical helmet. A protective metal helmet was, of course, worn by warriors. After the Greek conquest, Egyptian costume gradually became modified by foreign influences, although the extreme conservatism of the Egyptians preserved the ancient modes at least for ceremonial and religious ceremonies.

12, 14 Left and right, snake goddesses from the Palace of Knossos, Crete, *c.* 1600 BC

13 Above, *La Parisienne*. Fresco from Knossos, Crete, 1550–1450 BC

There is a curious modernity about these figures. With their tight waists and skirts *à la Polonaise* they suggest French fashions of the 1870s

Before we discuss 'classical' costume, however, it is necessary to consider the surprising clothes worn in Crete before the *Ills. 12–14* collapse of the Minoan civilization about the year 1400 BC. The very existence of this civilization was hardly suspected until the excavations of Sir Arthur Evans at the beginning of the present century revealed the richness of its artefacts and the elaboration of its clothes.

Crete seems to have been inhabited before the sixth millennium BC, but it was not until the beginning of the third millennium that a wave of immigrants from the Cyclades introduced a skill in navigation which enabled them to trade with Egypt and Asia Minor. It was inevitable that both these centres should influence the Cretans; but, at least from about 2000 BC, they developed a national style of striking originality.

From the costume point of view the most interesting period is the three and a half centuries which stretched from 1750 BC to 1400 BC. It was during this time that the Palace of Knossos was constructed, and it was from the excavations conducted there that most of our information is derived. The documentation consists of frescoes, painted pots and statuettes. Of these the last category is the most important, for the pots are not very numerous (compared with the large quantity that have come down to us from the 'classical' Greek period), and the frescoes are, naturally enough, in a poor state of repair and have not always been judiciously restored. With the clay figurines, however, we are on firm ground and they reveal an astonishing degree of luxury and refinement.

In a sense, of course, they are 'primitive' clothes in that male *Ill. 15* costume consists essentially of a loin-cloth, leaving the torso bare. Female costume shows a series of flounces with a tightly nipped-in waist and a corsage which terminates below the breasts. But the form of the male loin-cloth was much more varied than that of the Egyptian *schenti* and could consist of linen, wool or leather. For women the primitive loin-cloth had been lengthened to reach the ground and, by superimposing one piece of material over another, an effect was produced strangely similar to some of the European fashions of the late nineteenth century. The extremely tight waist accentuates this resemblance, and the result is so *chic*, in the modern sense, that one of the most attractive of the figures shown in the frescoes *Ill. 13* has been nicknamed *La Parisienne*.

The belts worn by men were sometimes adorned with metal plaques and sometimes made entirely of metal. The extreme slimness of the waist suggests that they were worn from early childhood. The metals used were gold, silver and bronze, and the belts composed of them are sometimes richly chased. In general men went bare-headed, although a kind of turban or bonnet was sometimes worn. Women, on the other hand, had the most elaborate headdresses, the hair being arranged in a variety of ways and surmounted by what may perhaps be regarded as the first 'smart hats' in the history of costume. Some of them are a curious anticipation of the hats worn by the Tanagra figurines of the Age of Pericles.

Ill. 16

The Cretans had a passion for bright colours such as red, yellow, blue and purple, as can be seen quite plainly in the frescoes that have been preserved. They were also extremely fond of jewellery, quantities of which have been discovered in the tombs of both men and women: rings, bracelets, collars, hair-pins. Rich people wore necklaces of lapis lazuli, agate, amethyst and rock-crystal mingled with pearls. The absence of fibulae should not cause surprise: such fastenings were not necessary for the *shaped* clothes of the Cretans as they were for the *draped* clothes of the Greeks. It is these 'classical' garments which we must now consider.

15 Priest-king from Knossos, Crete, 1550–1450 BC. Cretan men as well as women show the extremely constricted waist which could only have been attained by wearing a rigid girdle from childhood

16 Lady from Tanagra (right) and maid-servant from Alexandria, third century
B C. Over a tunic or *chiton*, women wore an enveloping mantle of linen or wool
similar to the male *himation*. The curious little hat worn by the lady was probably
made of plaited straw

Greeks and Romans

S CHOLARS now realize that the old 'classical' picture of Greece was much too simple. It was indeed bound to be so before the discovery of the Cretan civilization. It is true none the less that, from the period of the Dorian invasions of about 1200 BC, a new culture emerged which in manners and costume showed itself remarkably stable. Until the time of Alexander, in fact, there was no essential modification in the clothes worn by men or by women.

Greek costume during this long period had no form in itself. It was composed of rectangles of cloth of various sizes draped over the body without cutting or sewing the material. There could, of course, be considerable variation in the manner of adjustment, but the essential lines remained the same.

From the seventh to the first century B C both men and women wore the *chiton*, knee-length for men, ankle-length for women. Men, however, sometimes wore it long, as can be seen from the famous statue known as the 'Charioteer of Delphi'. It was *Ill. 18* kept in place by pins or brooches and was usually worn with a cord or belt round the waist. Scholars distinguish between the Doric and the Ionic *chiton*, the former being generally made of wool and the latter of linen. This being a more flexible material, it allowed a greater variety of folds, and the oblong of linen used was sometimes longer than the distance between the shoulders and the feet, enabling the cloth to be drawn up under the belt to form a kind of blouse.

It was at one time supposed that Greek clothes were white or of the natural colour of wool or flax, but this error derived from the fact that the antique statues discovered during the Renaissance had lost any colour they might have possessed. Further researches have shown that Greek garments were often coloured and patterned, except presumably those worn by the poor.

Some members of the lower classes dyed their garments a reddish brown, a practice apparently disapproved of by the authorities, for the historian Herodotus mentions an Athenian decree forbidding them to appear in dyed clothes at the theatre and in other public places. The upper classes were allowed more liberty, and it is said that the painter Polygnotus was the first to introduce brilliant colours such as red, yellow and purple. A polychrome statue recently discovered shows traces of green. The decoration of garments, often confined to the border, was embroidered rather than woven into the cloth and consisted of formal patterns such as the 'Greek fret', flowers and animal figures.

17 The goddess Athena, c. 450 B C. Greek costume was essentially drapery, a large rectangle of wool or linen being adjusted in various ways and held in place by one or two girdles, and by fibulae at the point of the shoulder

18 The Charioteer of Delphi, c. 475 B C. The long tunic or *chiton* was worn by both men and women, although for men it was a ceremonial garment, the short *chiton* being worn in ordinary life

19, 20 Outline drawings
of bas reliefs of the fifth
century BC

21 Right, maenad dancing.
Roman copy of Greek
original, late fifth century
BC

All these show the different
ways in which the rec-
tangle of cloth could be
adjusted round the body

The essential garment, the *chiton*, being a simple rectangle of cloth folded round the body, could be adjusted in various ways. Men could either fasten it with a brooch or pin on the left shoulder, leaving the right bare, or it could be fastened on both shoulders. It could be worn with one cord or belt round the waist or with two. No belt at all was worn before putting on a breastplate over it. In its later form the *chiton* was made of two pieces of cloth sewn together and was sometimes provided with sleeves.

Young men in general, and horsemen in particular, wore over the *chiton* a kind of short cloak, usually fastened on one *Ill. 23* shoulder and known as a *chlamys*. There was no impropriety in wearing the *chlamys* only, without the *chiton*, and in the gymnasium both sexes exercised naked: that, in fact, is what the word 'gymnasium' means. The Greeks, unlike their Semitic contemporaries, did not regard nudity as shameful. In cold weather a much larger cloak was worn: the *himation*. It could

24 Girl from Verona, Italy. Roman copy of a Greek original, 50 BC–AD 50. This represents a later and more sophisticated form of female Greek costume

22 Far left, torso of the goddess Minerva, mid fifth century BC

23 Left, boy wearing a *chlamys*, the short military cloak consisting, in this case, of a circular piece of material kept in place by a brooch on the right shoulder. Roman copy of Greek original of the first century BC

measure as much as eight feet by six. The female form of the *chlamys* was known as the *peplos* and, like its male counterpart, was worn over the *chiton*, which reached to the woman's feet. As luxury increased, it was sometimes made of very fine material, even of silk, in spite of repeated sumptuary laws which endeavoured to restrain the luxury of female garments. *Ill. 24* It should perhaps be noted here that luxury does not imply 'fashion'. The respectable Athenian lady was rarely seen abroad and had little temptation to compete with other women in striking or novel garments.

31

25 Head of an unknown woman from Sicily, sixth century BC

26 Head of the Muse Polyhymnia. Roman copy of Hellenistic original

27 Head of the Borghese Hera. Probably Roman copy of Greek original, third century BC

In the styles of hairdressing, however, we can trace considerable developments over the centuries. Before the Greek victories against the Persians, both men and women wore their hair long. Later, long hair was considered suitable only for boys or women. At puberty a boy cut off his hair and dedicated it to the gods.

Ill. 27 Even before the middle of the fifth century BC women sometimes bound their hair with a fillet. Afterwards this became the usual practice, and the back hair was sometimes enclosed in a kind of chignon worn low on the nape of the neck. Later still the back hair was fastened with ribbons in the form of a cone projecting behind the head. Wealthy women wore tiaras of gold and precious stones, and, after the Roman conquest, hair-styles became much more numerous and elaborate, with much use of frizzing and curling and the addition of artificial hair. Hats were used only for travelling, and even then were frequently worn on the shoulder rather than on the head. They were made of felt and had very broad brims. However, the Tanagra statuettes show that after the Mace-

donian conquest many women wore comical little hats, rather
like a miniature version of a Chinese hat, perched on the top
of their heads.

In general the Greeks were bearded up to the fifth century
B C, and even after that philosophers and other serious persons
kept up the old usage. Younger men shaved off all facial hair,
and the younger gods like Apollo and Mercury are always
depicted clean-shaven, the older ones like Jupiter and Vulcan
retaining their beards.

Indoors the Greeks rarely wore footgear of any kind, and the
poorer classes went barefoot even in the street. Even wealthy
people wore only sandals, although those of the courtesans
were sometimes gilded, the soles being studded with nails
arranged in such a way as to leave a footprint spelling out the
words 'Follow me'. (Such a sandal has actually been preserved.
It was found in Lower Egypt, but is thought by scholars to
have been similar to those worn by Greek courtesans.) The
sandals were attached to the feet and ankles by thongs tied in
many different ways, as innumerable statues testify.

33

28, 29 Warriors from vase-paintings, fifth century BC

Both figures are in armour, worn over the short tunic. The helmet of the second figure is the more characteristic. The shield, seen from the back, shows the method of holding it

The artists of the classical revival in the late eighteenth and early nineteenth centuries were persuaded – no doubt by the numerous nude statues in museums – that the Ancient Greeks went into battle naked, armed only with a sword, a shield and a helmet. In reality the Greek warriors protected themselves *Ill. 28* with tunics of leather reinforced with metal plaques, and wore greaves on their legs. The heavily armed infantry – the hoplites – and the cavalry wore in addition the characteristic Greek helmet which almost enclosed the head. It was sometimes provided with movable side pieces but had no visor, being *Ill. 29* merely pushed back on the head when not in use. The crest took the form of a horse's mane and was usually made of horsehair. The effect was singularly striking and beautiful. The

34

light infantry wore greaves of leather and tunics of doubled felt or leather with a metal belt. They also wore the *chlamys*, fastened on the shoulder or, in battle, rolled round the left arm to parry blows.

Just as archaeology has destroyed the long-accepted picture of Greek history, it has also modified our opinions of life during the first millennium BC in the Italian peninsula. So much was known of the Roman civilization that it was hardly realized how long a time elapsed before Rome became anything more than one small city-state struggling against its neighbours for survival and finally for dominance. Everybody knew that Rome had a king called Tarquin, but the implications of this were not so generally grasped: that the Romans at an early period of their development were ruled by a foreign dynasty, that of the Etruscans.

Who were the Etruscans? Scholars are still divided in their opinions. They are thought by some to have migrated from Asia, perhaps in successive waves, between the thirteenth and the eighth centuries BC. Others have thought that they represented an ethnic group of even earlier origin. They had connections with both Greece and Asia Minor, and their costume reflects both influences. Of this costume there is now a considerable documentation, mostly in the form of statues and bas-reliefs. Moreover, little as we know about their literature or their language, their recently discovered sculpture and wall-paintings enable us to reconstruct a fairly comprehensive picture of their mode of life.

Until their expansion into the southern part of Italy brought the Etruscans into contact with the Greek colonies of Magna Graecia, their garments showed little trace of Greek influence. Rather, they reflected an earlier connection with the Cretan civilization modified by Oriental elements. In a word, their costume was not draped. We can trace a certain evolution from *Ill. 30* what the scholars call a 'tunic-robe', characteristic of the period from about 700 BC to 575 BC, to a kind of toga made (like the

30 Female dancer, end of sixth century BC. Etruscan costume consisted of sewn garments, quite unlike the draperies of the Greeks

31 Dancers from the Tomb of the Leopards, Tarquinia. Etruscan, first quarter of fifth century B C

Roman toga which was derived from it) of a semicircle of cloth. *Ill. 31*
Sometimes it was rectangular and formed a kind of cloak. This
was worn by men, while women wore a long, tight-fitting
robe, without a girdle, with half-sleeves and sometimes slit at
the back, closed by ribbons when the garment had been put on
over the head. Over the robe was worn a long, rectangular
cloak which, when required, could be drawn over the head.

The most striking difference between Greek and Etruscan
costume was in the footwear. Until the fifth century B C, when
Greek influences caused them to adopt sandals, the Etruscans
wore a kind of high, laced boot with a turned-up toe, which was
obviously derived from the footwear of Asia Minor. But the
whole question of reciprocal influences is a field of study as yet
only partially explored. Once the Romans had established their
hegemony over the whole of Italy, they imposed their own way
of life and costume, and the very memory of a previous
Etruscan civilization faded away.

As we have seen, however, the Romans borrowed from the Etruscans one garment which became characteristically their *Ills. 32, 33* own: the toga. In its Roman form it grew ever more voluminous, required considerable skill in draping it about the body and effectively prevented any active pursuit. It was therefore essentially a garment for the upper classes, especially for senators, with whom it was always white. Until they attained puberty, free-born boys wore it with a purple border, when it was known as a *toga praetexta*, to be ceremonially exchanged for a white *toga virilis* when the time came. In mourning, a dark-coloured toga was worn and was sometimes draped over the head, as it was also for certain religious ceremonies. After about A D 100 the toga began to diminish in size, shrinking first to a *pallium* and then to a mere band of cloth, the stole. In the early days of the Republic, men wore a simple loin-cloth made of

32 Opposite, Vestal virgin. Roman, second century A D. On ceremonial occasions or in mourning a fold of cloth was drawn over the head

33 The Emperor Tiberius, first century A D. The Emperor is wearing the toga over a sleeved tunic

linen, this being replaced under the Empire by a sewn tunic, the equivalent of the Greek *chiton*. It consisted of two pieces of cloth sewn together, was put on over the head and gathered at the waist by means of a belt. It was knee-length, except on special occasions such as weddings, when it reached to the ground. It was worn under the toga by the upper classes; soldiers and workmen wore it as their sole garment. When provided with elbow-length sleeves it was known as a 'dalmatic', the name it continued to bear when, in a slightly modified form, it became one of the vestments of the Christian

39

Church. When it was embroidered all over it was called a *tunica palmata*. In pagan times it was worn, a little longer than knee-length, by the Roman dandies.

Sometimes two tunics were worn, the one next to the skin being the *subacula* and the over-tunic the *tunica exteriodum*. The latter grew gradually longer, reaching to the ankles from about AD 100. It was then known as a *caracalla*, and by AD 200 had been adopted by almost everyone.

At first the Romans, with their hardy traditions, strongly disapproved both of trews (to use the Scottish term) and of the long trousers worn by the barbarian tribes. But they gradually became accepted, being adopted first by soldiers.

At first the Romans were bearded, but from the second century BC they began to be clean-shaven, and this became the universal custom under the Empire until the time of Hadrian, who once more introduced beards. Hair was worn short, which

34 'Bikini girl' from Sicily, late third century AD. The Romans, unlike the Greeks, did not exercise in the gymnasium naked, but wore a modicum of clothing very similar to modern styles

35 Statues of the first century A D showing varieties of drapery. Centre, a priest offering a libation, with a fold of the toga drawn over his head

did not preclude considerable luxury, the dandies having their locks curled by means of hot tongs. In general the head was uncovered, but felt hats of various forms were sometimes worn: the rimless cap known as the *pileus*, a hat with a wide brim copied from the Greeks, and the soft Phrygian bonnet. The *cuculus* was a type of hood, sometimes attached to the cloak and sometimes forming a separate garment.

Women's clothes were at first very similar to those worn by men except for an unstiffened kind of bust-bodice known as the *strophium*. The tunic, however, was much longer than the masculine variety and formed a robe reaching to the feet. It was made first of wool, then of linen or cotton and finally, for the wealthy, of silk. The favourite colours were red, yellow and blue, and the garment was sometimes ornamented with a gold fringe and lavishly embroidered.

Ill. 34

41

36-9 Four heads showing the growing elaboration of hair-styles in the Roman period. Left, head of matron or widow. Right, Greek style

The *stola*, worn over the tunic, was a garment of similar shape but with sleeves, and over this was draped, for out of doors, a voluminous cloak, rather like the toga but rectangular in shape, known as the *pella*. In public it was usual for the head to be veiled. Hairdressing gradually grew more elaborate, and from the time of Messalina onwards it was impossible for a fashionable lady to dispense with the services of an *ornatrix*, who spent hours arranging the locks in a cone called a *tutulus* or surrounding the face with a frame of tight curls. Blonde hair was fashionable and, as we learn from Ovid, those who were naturally dark-haired resorted to bleaches. There was much use of false hair and even of entire wigs. The innumerable *Ills. 36-9* portrait-busts surviving from the later Empire show an enormous variety of styles, and it is evidence of the rapid changing of fashion that some ladies had their heads sculptured in two pieces so that the upper part, representing the hair, could be replaced, if desired, by a more fashionable coiffure.

42

Left, head showing Egyptian influence. Hellenistic. Right, head of a woman of the Flavian period, second century A D

All this was part of an increasing luxury, which satirists such as Juvenal seized upon as evidence of national decline. Jewellery of all kinds was increasingly worn. Simple head-bands were replaced by gold and silver tiaras encrusted with precious stones and cameos. Rings were worn by both sexes; the women added bracelets, anklets, necklaces and ear-rings. The poet Ovid mentions ear-rings made of three rows of pearls. Use was made of enamels and damascening, of ivory and cameos. Many of these artefacts came to Rome as the result of its conquests. Antioch and Alexandria were the principal centres of manufacture, but by the time of Augustus many articles were being made in Rome itself.

Decoration even spread to footwear, although this had originally been extremely simple: a sandal made of a single piece of untanned hide, overlapping the outline of the foot and kept in place by leather thongs. This was known as the *carbatina*, and in its slightly more sophisticated form as the *calceus*, and

43

was worn by the majority of Roman citizens. Slaves were forbidden to use it. Indoors women wore a kind of slipper called the *soccus*, which could be of various colours and was sometimes painted with patterns and even studded with precious stones after the manner of the *calceus patricius* worn by the Emperor Nero. Buskins, or closed boots, were sometimes used in bad weather. They were called *gallicae*, which is sufficient evidence that they had been borrowed from the Gauls.

Foreign influences of all kinds became more marked with the expansion of the Empire, especially with its expansion towards the east, until there was no luxury which the Roman patricians could not, if they wished, adopt. And then the centre of government itself moved east, with the establishment by Constantine of a new capital on the Bosphorus: Byzantium. And a new chapter opened in the history of Roman costume.

There had been a colony of Greeks on the European side of the Bosphorus since the seventh century BC, but for a thousand

40 Sarcophagus, late fourth century AD. The togas worn by these Christian Romans are markedly less ample than in previous centuries

41 Procession of female saints from Ravenna. Byzantine, c. 561

years it was little more than a village of reed huts and primitive fortifications. Then, in AD 330, the Emperor Constantine founded Byzantium on the site as his new capital. However, it did not long remain the capital of the whole Empire, which was divided by Theodosius the Great in AD 395 into the Eastern and Western Empires.

When the Western Empire fell in AD 476, Byzantium, or Constantinople as it was also called, was cut off from the West and became more and more affected by those Oriental influences which had been felt from its foundation. It could hardly have been otherwise, for its position made it the natural entrepôt of trade with the interior of Asia.

This naturally resulted in the evolution of quite a different kind of costume, a change neatly summed up by Carolyn G. Bradley: 'The simplicity of the old Roman dress gave way to the gay coloring, fringes, tassels and jewels of the East. The

Ill. 41

45

idea in dress in this era was to conceal and obscure the body' (*Western World Costume*, New York 1954). Constantine himself wore a costume very different from that of earlier Roman emperors. His robe of gold tissue was embroidered with floral patterns. Fastened to his shoulder by a jewelled brooch was a purple *chlamys*. A wide scarf called a *trabea* was crossed on his chest. The tunic had narrow sleeves, sometimes replaced by the wide-sleeved dalmatic, both encrusted with jewels as was also the *tablion*, an oblong panel on the front of the garment. Round his head he wore a band of material knotted at the back, but later emperors substituted a kind of crown, set with jewels and with strings of gems hanging from it on either side. This can be seen quite plainly in the splendid mosaics in the church of San Vitale in Ravenna. These show, in an elaborate frieze, the figures of the Emperor Justinian and his wife Theodora and are among the most valuable documents we possess of Byzantine costume at the height of its glory in the sixth century.

Ills. 42–4

One is struck at once by the *ecclesiastical* look of the Imperial garments. The Emperor was indeed a priest-king, the Viceroy of Christ on Earth. He did not actually say Mass, but he incensed the altar at sacred ceremonies, and it was he who called the Councils of the Church and, in some cases, presided over them. His whole life was regulated by liturgical requirements, all laid down with meticulous care in the *Book of Ceremonies* and, whenever he appeared in public, his clothes were not so much garments as 'vestments'. Similarly, the dress of all the courtiers and palace attendants was rigidly laid down in accordance with rank and function. In Byzantium as in Imperial China, all dress was 'hierarchical'. The 'Seduction Principle' was almost entirely absent, and the 'Utility Principle' completely ignored.

If, however, the Emperor was a priest-king he was also an Oriental potentate, a late echo of Darius 'King of Kings' and an early anticipation of the Turkish sultans who were later to rule in Constantinople. His palace was a strange mixture of monastery and seraglio, swarming with monks and eunuchs.

46

Another Oriental touch was the method of selecting an Empress. It resolved itself into a kind of beauty competition, girls being brought from every part of the Empire. Their rank does not seem to have mattered, and when the candidates had been screened and only the most beautiful remained, the Emperor himself made the final choice, presenting the girl with an apple. Fantastic as it may seem, it was in this manner that Justinian selected Theodora. She was of humble origin, her father being in charge of the bears used in bear-baiting. But in Theodora's case there was another difficulty: she was an actress and dancer, professions of which the Church strongly disapproved. Special legislation had to be enacted in order to allow her to marry Justinian.

Once elevated to the purple, she showed herself a woman of great courage and indomitable will. She made an admirable consort. She was, of course, surrounded by all the ecclesiastical pomp that surrounded her husband, and her appearance, like his, is preserved for posterity in the gleaming mosaics of San Vitale. She wore a long white tunic adorned with a vertical band covered with embroideries. Another band, called a *maniakis*, embroidered with gold thread and set with precious stones and pearls, was draped over her shoulders. In addition she wore a short-sleeved robe, with a jewelled belt and fringes at the hem, and a purple cloak embroidered with figures of the Magi. On her head she had an even more splendid diadem than the Emperor's. This was the *stephanos*, set with precious stones and with long strings of pearls hanging down on either side. On her feet were closed shoes of soft leather, coloured red and enriched with embroideries.

The materials used were rich and varied, as may be gathered from the fragments that have survived, mostly as ecclesiastical vestments or the wrappings of relics. Wool, which had been the textile most in use in the early days of the Empire, was laid aside in favour of cotton and fine linens from Egypt and silk from China. The latter had at first to be transported by caravan across the whole width of Asia, a lengthy and costly business.

And then, according to the legend, two missionary monks
Ill. 44 were dispatched by Theodora herself to China and returned
bringing with them a number of silkworms in a hollow cane.
This, perhaps, is the first example in history of industrial
espionage. In any case, the silkworms flourished and multiplied
and Byzantium was able to spin and weave its own silk cloth.

The most striking thing about the costume of New Rome
as opposed to that of Old Rome was its colour. Purple was
reserved for the Imperial couple but all other colours were
employed in the clothes of the rich. Many garments were
heavily patterned with animals, flowers and Biblical scenes. It
is recorded that one Byzantine senator had on his toga a complete series of pictures representing the life of Christ. This
emphasizes once more the close connection, unknown perhaps
at any other period of history, between ecclesiastical and civil
costume.

It is impossible to record here all the modifications which
occurred in Byzantine costume over the centuries. It is sufficient
to note that they nearly all provide evidence of increasing
Orientalization. In the twelfth century the Persian *caftan* was
adopted, as well as a mantle buttoned down the front. The
open coronet of Justinian was exchanged for a closed crown
called a *camelaukion*. From Assyria was derived the long-
sleeved *granatza*, a robe reaching to the ground. From the sixth
century turbans were sometimes worn, and scholars have noted,
between the seventh and ninth centuries, a Chinese influence
on hats.

But if Byzantine costume was affected by foreign influences,
it in its turn was much imitated in surrounding districts. Even
after the fall of Constantinople, Bulgarian kings wore clothes
of Byzantine derivation and the rulers of Muscovy continued
to do so until the seventeenth century, when Peter the Great
broke with tradition and turned Russia's face to the West. And,
of course, the Orthodox Church continues to this day to per-
form its ceremonies in vestments not essentially different from
those worn by the Byzantine emperors.

48

42–44 Byzantine splendour: the Empress Theodora and her suite, 500–526.
Above left, Theodora's husband, the Emperor Justinian

CHAPTER THREE

The Dark Ages and the Middle Ages

THROUGHOUT its history the Roman State was surrounded
by barbarian peoples who lived beyond the borders of its
dominion, and sometimes their incursions were dangerous
indeed. As early as the second century BC, a Roman army had
been defeated by a people they identified as Teutoni or Teutons.

At this period the Teutons were primitive enough. Their
principal garment seems to have consisted of a short tunic
formed of two pieces of leather sewn together. Later it was
made of wool or linen. Under the tunic were worn breeches
or baggy trousers, which in Roman eyes was the very mark of
the barbarian. Naturally, the Teutons were influenced by their
contacts with Rome, and they gradually adopted something
resembling Roman costume but made, in general, of coarser
materials such as hemp.

By the end of the first century AD, another northern tribe,
the Goths (originally of Scandinavian origin), had settled in
what was, until 1945, East Prussia, and they, too, threatened the
Roman civilization. As Ostrogoths they pushed eastward into
what is now Russia; as Visigoths they pushed westward into
Spain and other regions, sacking Rome under their great
leader Alaric in the fifth century; and as Langobards or Lom-
bards they firmly established themselves in northern Italy. From
the descriptions of such Roman historians as Sidonius Apol-
linaris we know that they wore sleeved tunics of linen, edged
with fur, and became gradually Romanized.

New waves of invasion from the east threatened the Teutonic
tribes themselves. The Huns came originally from Mongolia;
by the middle of the first century AD they had reached Europe,
and by the fourth century, under Attila, Rome itself.

In France the Gauls had adopted not only Roman dress and customs but the Latin language. Like the Britons they had (in the upper classes at least) become completely Romanized. But Gaul was successfully invaded by the Franks (i.e. the Teutons) from across the Rhine, and by the fifth century A D the Frankish dynasty of the Merovingians had established itself over the greater part of the country.

We would know much less of the costume of the Merovingian period in France (A D 481–752) if it were not for the fact that the invading Franks who now controlled the country were in the habit of burying their dead, instead of burning their bodies as the Romanized Gauls had done. Buried with the corpses of kings or other distinguished persons were the clothes, arms and accoutrements they had used in life. Excavations in Lorraine and at Le Mans have yielded specimens of fine linen garments which, although fragmentary, show that it was usual to wear a knee-length tunic called a *gonelle*, embroidered at the edge and caught in at the waist with a belt. In battle the tunic would be made of stout material, or of leather, and covered with metal plaques. The men of this period wore *braies* or breeches, sometimes ending at the knee and leaving the legs bare, sometimes long and cross-gartered.

Little is known of female costume at this period, since women are poorly represented in the burials. We know, however, from other sources, that they generally wore a long tunic called a *stola* decorated with embroidered bands. The arms were bare. Brooches kept the garment in place on the shoulders, and the waist was encircled with a leather belt. A kind of scarf, called a *palla,* was draped over the shoulders.

Fortunately, one quite recent discovery, in the church of Saint-Denis, near Paris, gives more exact information. Fragments of material from the tomb of a Merovingian queen, Arnegonde (A D 550–70), show that she was buried in a chemise of fine linen with a violet silk robe over it. Over this was a long tunic of red silk, open in front and with long wide sleeves. A wide belt, crossed at the back and tied low in front, kept the tunic in place, and attached to the tunic by richly enamelled gold fibulae was a waist-length veil. The closed shoes were of black leather with laces long enough to be crossed over the leg to the height of the garter.

Neither men nor women seem to have worn hats. Both sexes had long hair, men and young girls wearing it loose, and married women binding it into a kind of chignon. The latter covered the head with a veil, either in the form of a turban or long enough to cover the entire body.

When the Merovingians were succeeded by the Carolingians (AD 752–987), conditions in France and in Western Europe generally were rather more settled and luxury increased. Charlemagne became ruler of the Franks, controlling, in AD 771, territory corresponding roughly to France and Germany; and in AD 800 he was crowned in Rome as Emperor. We have a detailed description of his costume from the hand of his secretary Eginhard, but we must be careful to distinguish between his ordinary dress and the clothes he felt compelled to wear as Roman Emperor. The latter were of extreme magnificence and were plainly derived from the Court dress of Byzantium. This was not only a matter of cut: the actual materials were almost certainly imported from the Near East. Fragments are still preserved of the clothes in which he was buried at Aachen and we have records of the complete garments found when his tomb was opened in the twelfth century.

Over a tunic with sleeves edged with gold he wore a dalmatic, and over this a number of garments, including one of brocade manufactured in Constantinople, figured with elephants in floriated circles of green, blue and gold, and one of cloth-of-gold, brocaded in squares with a ruby in the centre of each. His shoes were of scarlet leather embroidered with gold and set with emeralds. On his head he wore a splendid gold crown set with jewels and enamelled plaques.

Eginhard tells us that his habitual costume was much simpler, consisting of an under-tunic of linen or wool and over it a tunic with a border of coloured silk. Over this again he wore,

45 The four parts of the Empire (Sclavinia, Germania, Gallia and Roma) paying homage to Otto III; right, the Emperor Otto enthroned, 997–1000. The miniature shows the bright colours worn in the period

attached to his left shoulder by means of a brooch, a short semi-circular cloak, lined with fur in winter. He had *braies* or breeches cross-gartered to below the knee, and on his head a round cloth cap with an embroidered border.

In England, Charlemagne's contemporary, Offa, King of Mercia, and the kings who followed him, seem to have worn quite simple garments. We know, from an illuminated manuscript preserved in the library of Corpus Christi College, Cambridge, that King Athelstan wore a short yellow tunic with a narrow gold border, a blue cloak and red hose; and we know from an illuminated grant of lands to the Abbey of Winchester (AD 966) that King Edgar was similarly clad, except that his tunic was shorter and his legs enclosed in narrow bands like puttees.

We have considerable information, again from illuminated manuscripts, about the dress of Anglo-Saxon women. The principal garments were the tunic or kirtle, worn over a smock

53

and put on over the head; the super-tunic or roc, also put on over the head and sometimes hitched up over the girdle to show the garment beneath (it had embroidered borders at neck, hem and sleeves); and the mantle, sometimes as long as the tunic and fastened under the chin. The hair was concealed by a veil or 'head-rail', long enough to be crossed over the bosom and hang down to the knees.

The coming of the Danes made very little difference to costume in England, except that the Danish men wore their hair longer and were much given to the wearing of bracelets, which were regarded as marks of military prowess. The Norman Conquest, however, was quite a different matter, for the descendants of the Norsemen who had established themselves in Normandy were, by this time, completely Frenchified, having even abandoned the language of their forefathers. Edward the Confessor, who ascended the throne in 1042, was himself half Norman, and even Harold, who succeeded him, had spent long periods in France. The monkish chroniclers of the time were already complaining that the English had forgotten their usual simplicity, had trimmed their hair, shortened their tunics and generally adopted French modes.

Nevertheless, there was sufficient difference for the English spies who were sent out before the Battle of Hastings to report that the invading army consisted of nothing but priests, that is, men with short hair, the back of the neck being shaved. It was to celebrate this battle that Queen Matilda and her ladies embroidered the long strip of linen, wrongly called a tapestry, which is still preserved at Bayeux and which serves as an admirable illustration of the costume of the period. We see King *Ill. 46* Edward in his long tunic receiving messengers in tunics shorter than knee-length, and over them the super-tunic, which was a loose, circular garment put on over the head. Stockings had ornamented tops, visible below the tunic and allowed to wrinkle so that they look very much like the leg-bandages already described. Leg-bandages were also worn, bound either spirally or criss-cross over the stockings.

54

46 King Edward the Confessor, from the Bayeux tapestry. Late eleventh century

47 Scene from a play by Terence, derived from a Carolingian manuscript. This bears witness to the comparatively static forms of costume over several centuries

Scholars have long been aware of the influence of the Crusades in modifying the costume of Western Europe. It is true that already before the eleventh century there was contact with the Mohammedan world through Sicily and Spain, and the rich stuffs of the Orient had thus found their way to the West, but only in very small quantities and out of reach of all but wealthy kings. When the Normans captured Sicily in 1060, they found a civilization vastly superior to their own in learning and craftsmanship, and a degree of luxury unknown to them before. Many of the craftsmen remained under their new rulers and were eagerly employed by them in weaving and goldsmiths' work. This patronage continued when Frederick of Hohenstaufen, crowned as Holy Roman Emperor in 1220, established his Court at Palermo. Under his tolerant rule all the arts flourished and he was himself, in his tastes and his garments, more like an Oriental sultan than a Christian king.

In Spain the gradual conquest of the lands occupied by the Moors resulted in the capture of rich booty: jewellery and fine tissues far more luxurious than the contemporary products of Christian Europe. Then came the Crusades and the reopening of trade with the Near East. But the returning Crusaders brought back with them not only Oriental materials but the clothes themselves, or a knowledge of their cut. Western ladies adopted the Mohammedan veil, or a least a wimple concealing the lower part of the face. On the other hand, they began to mould their gowns to the figure by means of buttons down the side, the upper part of the gown being thus drawn tight over the bust. The sleeves became immensely long and very wide at the wrist, as can be seen in one of the most valuable documents of the period, the *Hortus Deliciarum* of the Abbess of Landsberg in Alsace, which was produced in about 1175. Another valuable source of information is to be found in the

Ills. 49–51 sculptures of the cathedrals which began to be erected in France and Germany in the twelfth century.

Part of the confusion in descriptions of medieval costume is due to the failure to distinguish between hose and breeches.

56

48 Crusader doing homage, thirteenth century

Even such established historians of costume as Hottenroth, Viollet-le-Duc and Racinet have failed to do this, and it was not until quite recent years that the distinction was made plain by writers like Dorothy Hartley and C. Willett Cunnington.

In the eleventh century breeches or *braies* were ankle-length trousers kept in place by a cord threaded through the top, rather low over the hips. The nobility wore them fitted to the leg, the lower classes loose and rather baggy. They were sometimes worn with leg-bandages bound spirally or in a criss-cross pattern. Hose, or *chausses* (i.e. stockings), were cut to the shape of the leg out of wool or linen cloth, knitting being practically unknown in England until the reign of Elizabeth I. In the eleventh century they reached to just below the knee, with a patterned top, rather like that of modern golfing stockings. But in the twelfth century they rose to mid-thigh, being made wide enough at the top to be pulled over the *braies*. Some ended at the ankles, some had a strip like a stirrup under the instep and some were provided with a thin leather sole obviating the use of shoes indoors. They were sometimes striped and brightly coloured. Meanwhile, the breeches were shrinking to become invisible drawers. With labourers at work they became a mere breech-clout.

49 Shepherds, from Chartres Cathedral, *c.* 1150. They wear the short tunics of the common people and leg-coverings made of narrow bands of material

50 A sainted king and queen, from
Chartres Cathedral, *c.* 1150. The
long, open sleeves should be noted

51 The Lady Uta, one of the
founder-figures in Naumburg
Cathedral, *c.* 1245

52 Scene showing peasant costume, *c.* 1335–40

The twelfth century showed little essential modification, except that the tunic was more closely fitting and sleeves showed a sudden widening at the wrist. The hood, which originally had formed part of the cloak, became a separate garment in the second half of the century, with a small shoulder-length cape attached to it. There were several forms of hat, ranging from *Ill. 52* the pointed 'Phrygian' cap to something resembling a beret, and to hats with wide brims which were worn over the hood when travelling. Indoors, men sometimes wore the coif of plain linen covering the ears and tied under the chin.

In female dress a new style appeared about 1130, the bodice of the gown, at least for the upper classes, being moulded so as to fit tightly down to the hips, the skirt below that being cut wide and falling in folds to the feet. It was sometimes sufficiently *Ill. 53* long to form a train. The super-tunic also was more closely fitting and with wider sleeves. The veil was sometimes kept in place by a half-circle or complete circle of gold worn round the forehead. In addition, from the late twelfth century to the early fourteenth century, the barbette was worn. This was a

60

53 The elaborate clothes of a knight and his lady, *c.* 1335–40

54, 55, 56 Brass-rubbings from sepulchral monuments, dated 1375, 1391 and 1430

linen band passing under the chin and drawn up over the temples. Worn during the same period was the wimple or gorget. It was made of fine white linen or silk, covered the neck and part of the bosom, and was sometimes tucked into the top of the gown, the ends being then drawn up and pinned to the top of the head under the veil to frame the face.

It was in the second half of the fourteenth century that clothes both for men and for women took on new forms, and something emerges which we can already call 'fashion'. The old *gipon*, which was beginning to be called a 'doublet', was padded in the front to swell out the chest and was worn much shorter, so short indeed that the moralists of the period

57, 58, 59 Rubbings dated 1437, *c.* 1480 and *c.* 1501. The ladies' headdresses show a growing elaboration in the late fourteenth and fifteenth centuries

denounced it as indecent. It was worn very tight, with buttons down the front and with a belt low over the hips.

The upper classes wore over the *gipon* a garment known as a *cote-hardie*. This was the super-tunic of a previous age, but it was now low-necked and tight-fitting and buttoned down the front. The *cote-hardie* of the lower classes was looser and, having no buttons, was put on over the head. The length of the fashionable *cote-hardie* gradually diminished and the edge was often dagged – that is, cut in curious patterns. The sleeves were tight to the elbow but then flared out, becoming wide enough to hang down to the knees or even lower. About 1375 the *cote-hardie* began to have a collar.

Ill. 54

63

A characteristic garment from about 1380 to 1450 was the *houppelande*, later to be known as the 'gown'. It fitted the shoulders and was loose below, with a belt at the waist. Its length varied, being longest for ceremonial occasions. The sleeves were extremely wide and sometimes so long as to reach to the ground. It had a high upright collar, sometimes reaching to the ears, and its edge was dagged into fantastic shapes. Chaucer, in *The Parson's Tale*, blames 'so much pouncing of chisel to make holes, so much dagging of shears, with the superfluity in length of the aforesaid gowns, trailing in the dung and in the mire, on horse and eke on foot, as well of man as of woman'.

Women, in general, were less extravagantly clad than men, so far as the shape of their garments was concerned. The main item of their dress was the kirtle or gown, close-fitting down to the waist and then flaring out in a full skirt hanging in folds. The sleeves were so tight-fitting that they had to be buttoned over the lower area and were sufficiently long to extend over half the hand. Over the gown was worn the *cote-hardie*, similar to that worn by men. The sleeves had long streamers or tippets *Ill. 60* which sometimes trailed on the ground. From the middle of the fourteenth century it was fashionable to wear the sideless sur-coat, a curious garment with large openings at the sides. The front formed a kind of stiffened stomacher known as a 'plackard'.

The effect was of tight lacing – one of the most potent weapons of fashion through the ages – which now, for the first time, began to be exploited. Another innovation, with an even greater erotic appeal, was décolletage, the cutting away of the top of the robe to reveal part of the bosom. Yet another was the abandonment of the veil, which henceforward was worn only by nuns and widows. Instead there began a long series of headdresses, growing ever more elaborate and fantastic until the end of the fifteenth century.

Ills. 54–9 We can watch this development in tomb sculptures, and in particular in the memorial tablet known as a 'brass'. This was a sheet of brass cut out in the shape of a figure and engraved with

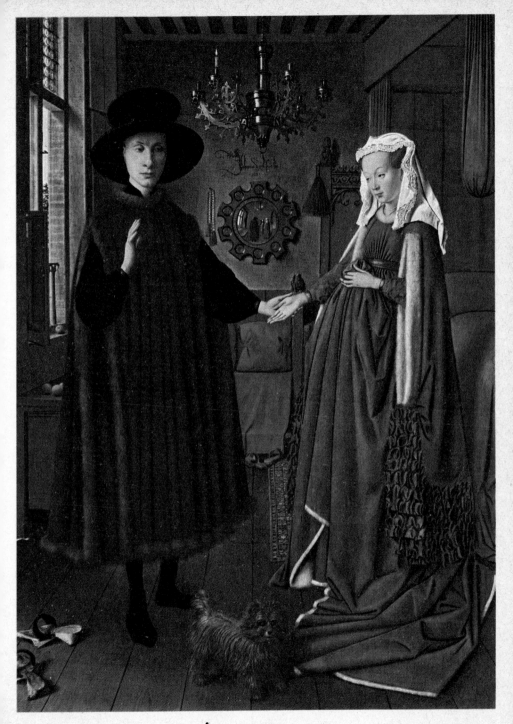

60 *The Marriage of Giovanni (?) Arnolfini and Giovanna Cenami(?)*, by Jan van Eyck, 1434

details of the costume of the deceased, and let in to the pavement of a church. Curiously enough such memorials are to be found only in England and in certain parts of Flanders. They are a most valuable source of documentation, since it is easy to take rubbings from them, and such rubbings might almost be called the fashion plates of the later Middle Ages. Above all, they have the inestimable advantage of being dated.

Already, towards the end of the thirteenth century, the crespine had made its appearance, worn with the barbette and the fillet. This was a kind of hairnet, and was a somewhat startling innovation, since previous ages had considered visible female hair to be immoral. The next stage was to wear the crespine by itself, the alternative being vertical plaits on each side of the face. These are very characteristic of the last quarter of the fourteenth century. At the same period the veil reappeared, but in a new form. This was the goffered veil or 'nebula' headdress, made of a half-circle of linen framing the face. Sometimes it was composed of several layers and resembled the ruff of the second half of the sixteenth century, except that, of course, it was worn not round the neck but round the face. The fillet also took on a new shape, forming two hollow ornamental pillars through which the hair was drawn. The effect, in contrast to that of the rounded 'nebula' headdress, was extremely square, the face being, as it were, enclosed in a frame.

Towards the end of the fourteenth century appeared also the 'cushion' headdress, which was a kind of padded roll worn over a hairnet. The hair was coiled above each ear in small *Ill. 68* knobs known as 'templers'. For the first third of the fifteenth century the effect was one of breadth. Sometimes this was pushed to an extreme, the width of the two templers combined being twice that of the face.

The horned headdress which came in about 1410 had a wire structure like the horns of a cow on which was draped the veil. This was followed by the heart-shaped headdress, the name itself being a sufficient description. Both of these styles were

66

61, 62 Engravings by Israel van Meckenem showing the transition from the pointed shoe (*c.* 1470) to the broad shoe (*c.* 1485)

attempts to use the veil as a decorative attraction, the opposite of its original purpose. To this extent the denunciations of contemporary moralists may seem justified.

The second half of the century saw a number of new varieties. Instead of being broad, headdresses tended to be high, sometimes extremely so. The sausage-shaped roll of padded material forming a narrow U over the forehead, known in a primitive form to the previous generation, was now much elongated and tilted backward. The same happened to the 'turban' headdress and the 'chimney-pot' headdress. (These are not contemporary names but attempts by modern scholars at descriptive labels.) The latter had a veil attached to the top.

The *hennin* or 'steeple' headdress was much worn in France. In England it took the shape of a truncated cone and was therefore not very different from the 'chimney-pot' headdress. A better name, perhaps, would be 'flower-pot'. Most spectacular of all was the 'butterfly' headdress. This was a wire structure attached to a small cap or caul in which the hair was enclosed. It rose high above the head and supported a diaphanous veil in the shape of a butterfly's wings. It was a very popular fashion up to about 1485.

Men's clothes in the second half of the fifteenth century showed a number of developments. The main garment was still the doublet, but it could be worn extremely short, so short as to demand the use of a codpiece at times. It began to develop

63 *Wedding of Boccaccio Adimari*. Florentine, *c.* 1470. Probably from a *cassone* or dower-chest. The men's headgear shows the transition from cowl (into which the head was inserted) to hat

a high stand-up collar. The *cote-hardie* was replaced by the jacket or jerkin, increasingly tight-fitting, and the shoulders were padded to increase the apparent width of the body. The sleeves were generally full and sometimes detachable.

The *houppelande* was now called the 'gown' and was worn by older men, doctors, magistrates and the like. It fell in vertical pleats to the ankles and was fastened down the front with hooks and eyes. It was worn with or without a belt, and the sleeves were usually very full. When they hung low down they were known as 'surplice sleeves'. It was usual to line the gown, sometimes with fur.

There was considerable variety in male headgear. Until about 1380 the hood with long liripipe had been almost universally worn. Then someone had the bright idea of sticking his *head* into the opening where his face should have been, winding the hood, with its dagged edge, round the head in the form of a turban and tying it in place with the liripipe. Philip the Good is shown wearing a headdress of this type.

A development from this was the *chaperon*, which consisted of a circular padded roll to which was attached a gorget consisting of folds of material cut in decorative shapes. The effect was rather similar to that of the turban already described, but it was, so to speak, 'ready-made', required no arranging and

Ills. 63, 67

70

64 *Duchess of Urbino*, by Piero della Francesca (after 1473)

65 *Portrait of a lady in red.* Florentine, *c.* 1470.

66 *Margaret of Denmark, Queen of Scotland*, ascribed to Hugo van der Goes, 1476

It is thought that the eyebrows and hair on the forehead were shaved in imitation of classical sculpture

could be put on and off without difficulty. It had a strange history. It was sometimes worn on the shoulder instead of the head, and in this position shrank and became a badge of livery. In its final term it became the cockade on the nineteenth-century coachman's hat.

During the fifteenth century hats were increasingly worn, and assumed many different shapes. Some had flat crowns and narrow brims, some were very tall and had no brims. Crowns tapered or ballooned out. Something resembling the Turkish fez (and frequently red in colour) can be seen in contemporary paintings. Some hats were not unlike the modern bowler, some were adorned with plumes. Towards the end of the century a flat cap was worn, with a turned-up brim adorned with a single jewelled ornament.

Until the 1480s men's shoes were markedly pointed, some-times fantastically so. This tendency had been seen as early as 1360 and was regarded with disfavour by the ecclesiastical and

71

civil authorities. King Edward III even enacted a sumptuary law which laid down that 'no Knight under the estate of a lord, esquire or gentleman, nor any other person, shall wear any shoes or boots having spikes or points exceeding the length of two inches, under the forfeiture of forty pence'. This, like all sumptuary laws, was completely ineffective, for in the following reign, the 'spikes or points' sometimes reached the length of eighteen inches or more. Such shoes were known as *crackowes*, or *poulaines*, the terms being corruptions, respectively, of Cracow and Poland. Poland was then part of the Kingdom of Bohemia, and the names are explained by the fact that King Richard II married Anne of Bohemia and the gentlemen who came in her suite to England wore shoes with extremely pointed toes. The extreme fashion lasted until about 1410, and pointed shoes of some kind until the advent of the Tudors. The revolution in fashion this implied is dealt with in the next chapter.

67 Philip the Good, Duke of Burgundy, receiving a copy of the *Chroniques de Hainaut*. Flemish, 1448

68 Christine de Pisan presenting her book of poems to Isabel of Bavaria, Queen of France. French, early fifteenth century. The ladies' headdresses are of two kinds: *à cornes*, and with the veil raised from the face by means of pins

69 Extreme form of the *poulaine* or *crackowe*, from the *Chronique d'Angleterre*. Flemish, fifteenth century

CHAPTER FOUR

The Renaissance and the sixteenth century

THE FASHIONS, and art forms generally, of the Gothic North had never been fully accepted in Italy, and by the middle of the fifteenth century Italian modes had already diverged consider- ably from those of the rest of medieval Europe. In their style of headdress, for example, the fine ladies painted by Van der
Ill. 70 Weyden in the Netherlands and those painted in Italy by
Ill. 71 Ghirlandaio could hardly be more different. On the one hand, the towering line of the *hennin*; on the other, the hair exposed and dressed close to the head, with side curls and a bun at the back. There was much difference also in the cut of the sleeves, close-fitting in the North, swelling out in Italy, with slashes through which the white chemise could be seen. Often the sleeves were made detachable, and were heavily decorated – a reflection of the enormous increase in luxury brought about by the mercantile prosperity of the Italian cities.

The invasion of Italy by the French King Charles VIII doubt- less introduced the Italians to French fashions, but in general the influence was the other way. The Renaissance was, so to speak, transplanted over the Alps, and if Charles VIII was still
Ill. 80 a medieval king, Francis I was a Renaissance monarch.

So, in England, was Henry VIII. It is true that the reign of his father, Henry VII, had already seen many modifications in medieval costume. The line, instead of being vertical, was now horizontal; the shoes, instead of being excessively pointed, became broad-toed, as if to echo the new style of architecture with its flattened arch. Ladies' headdresses ceased to be replicas of Gothic pinnacles and began to resemble Tudor windows. And with the advent of the new century a curious Germanism

70 *Portrait of a lady*, by Rogier van der Weyden, *c.* 1455

71 *Giovanna Tornabuoni*, by Domenico Ghirlandaio, 1488

72 *Nuremberg housewife and Venetian lady*. Drawing by Dürer, 1495.

These show the marked contrast in hairdressing and clothes between the styles of northern Europe and Italy

Venedig
Maylanð
Offen
Inſprueck
Nürmberg
Craca
Antorff
Liſbona

PER · IACOB · FVGGER
recht con   no faſt

75 The Swiss Guards. Detail from the *Mass of Bolsena*, by Raphael, 1511–14

73 Jacob Fugger 'the Rich', the Emperor's banker, with Matthäus Schwarz, his chief accountant, 1519

74 German *Landsknecht*, *c.* 1530. An example in their extreme form of the slashings worn by the German mercenaries but influencing male costume all over Europe

76

began to influence the dress of the fashionable in both France and England.

Much has been written about this strange development, but contemporary chroniclers are almost unanimous in ascribing it to the victory of the Swiss over Charles the Bold, Duke of

Burgundy, at the Battle of Grandson (1476). Much plunder of silk and other costly materials fell to the victors, who slashed the booty to pieces and used it to patch their own ragged clothes. The Swiss troops were copied by the German mercenaries, and from them the fashion spread to the French Court, probably introduced by the Guise family, itself half German. The marriage of Henry VII's sister Mary to Louis XII of France caused the English to adopt the *landsknecht* fashion also.

Ill. 76   Slashing indeed (i.e. the practice of cutting slits in the material of garments and pulling the lining through) became almost universal in the early 1500s; but it was in Germany that it reached its most extravagant extreme. For not only the doublet but the breeches were slashed; indeed, quite literally, 'cut to ribbons'. Nether garments consisted of broad bands of material falling to the knees and sometimes to the ankles. Care was taken that the bands on each leg should form different patterns, and they could even be of different colours. We hear in the chronicles of 'hose made in the German manner, the

76, 77 *Duke Henry of Saxony and his wife*, by Lucas Cranach, 1514. The slashing in men's clothes was matched by the rich decoration of women's garments

78, 79 Two stages in the development of the ruff: left, *Katherina Knoblau-chin*, by Conrad Faber, 1532. Right, *Portrait of an unknown man*, by Bartolommeo Veneto, before 1540

one [leg] yellow, the other black, slashed with sixteen ells of taffeta'.

Slashing spread to women's clothes, but never reached such extravagant lengths. It is obvious that whereas breeches could be slashed, skirts were not susceptible to such treatment. Indeed, female dress at this period is much more modest than male costume. Skirts, however, were ampler and more richly embroidered than in earlier reigns. Over the kirtle, which consisted of a skirt and bodice sewn together, was worn the gown, falling in ample folds to the ground from a tight-fitting waist. The sleeves ceased to be tight and became very large indeed, with a deep turn-back of fur, as can be seen in Holbein's portraits. There was much use of fur both by men and by women: lynx, wolf and sable being the favourites. The neck was cut square and low, and above it could be seen the top of the chemise. Men also, in the early years of the century, were

Ill. 77

Ills. 81–2

79

80 *Francis I of France*. Attributed to François Clouet. Early sixteenth century

81, 82 *Helen of Bavaria*, by Hans Schöpfer, *c.* 1563–6, and *Jane Seymour*, *c.* 1536–7, by Holbein. These two illustrations show the square décolletage and the contrast between the German and English modes of headgear

décolleté, with the top of the shirt showing. Through this was **Ills. 79, 80** threaded a string, and when this was drawn tight we can already see the beginnings of what was to be the ruff of the second half of the century.

The main male garment was the doublet, sometimes long enough to fall to the knee. It had an opening in the front through which could be seen the codpiece. The sleeves grew gradually **Ill. 83** wider and were often paned or slashed. Sometimes double sleeves were worn, one pair hanging loose and of a different colour. The materials most in favour were velvet, satin and cloth-of-gold. We know from his Wardrobe Account that Henry VIII possessed a doublet of purple satin, embroidered with gold and silver thread and sewn all over with pearls. Over the doublet was worn the jacket or jerkin, either double

83 *Henry VIII.*
School of
Holbein. The
acme of
masculinity in
dress with wide
shoulders and a
codpiece

breasted or closed down the front with laces or buttons; over
this was the gown, fitting loosely over the shoulders, falling in
ample folds to the feet and usually edged with fur.

The nether garments consisted of breeches and stockings
sewn together. The top edge was secured to the doublet by
means of points, i.e. laces threaded through eyelet holes in both
garments and tied in small bows. These points were made of
linen or silk thread lipped with metal tags, known as 'aiglets'.
The shoes were at first extremely broad, in the shape called

'duck-bill'. The heels were flat, the soles of leather or cork, *Ill. 83* the uppers of leather, velvet or silk. Shoes were often slashed and adorned with jewels.

Hats were worn indoors as well as out, and for the most part took the form of a soft, low bonnet. Sometimes this had a brim which could be turned up in front and kept in place by a jewel; or the brim could be cut away in the front, but with side pieces which could be turned down over the ears. The brim was sometimes slashed in various patterns. A wide-brimmed hat was worn by travellers and country folk. A curious survival from the medieval period was the linen coif tied under the chin. In the sixteenth century its use was confined to the elderly or to lawyers and other professional men. Men wore their hair long, and under Henry VII and in the early years of Henry VIII's reign had clean-shaven faces. But in 1535, according to Stow's *Annals*, 'The King commanded all about his Court to poll

84 Costume plate by Jost Amman showing German bourgeois dress, *c.* 1560

their heads, and to give them example, he caused his own head to be polled, and from henceforth his beard to be . . . no more shaven.' It is thought that, in this, he was following the fashion inaugurated by the French King Francis I.

Some of the greatest portraits of all time were painted in the sixteenth century: one has only to mention the names of Holbein, Bronzino, Titian. But for the most part these artists painted very grand people in their very grandest clothes. For *Ill. 84* the physical appearance of the less exalted we must turn to German *Kleinmeister* such as Aldegrever, the Beham brothers,

85 Opposite, *The Ambassadors*, by Holbein, 1533

86 *Thomas Cranmer*, by Gerhardt Flicke, 1546

Jost Amman and Virgil Solis. The Behams show us the peasants, Aldegrever the patricians, while Jost Amman plunges us right into the everyday life of the middle classes.

Naturally, these peasant and middle-class garments exhibited none of the extravagance of those worn in Court circles. But every prosperous citizen possessed what the Germans called a *Schaube*, an overcoat shaped like a cassock but generally without sleeves. If it had sleeves, they hung empty behind the visible sleeves of the garment worn underneath. The *Schaube*, often lined with fur, became the typical garment of the scholar. Luther wore one and thereby dictated the costume of the Lutheran clergy to the present day. In England Thomas Cranmer wore a similar garment, and this, with the chain round the neck, became the ancestor of the accepted costume of mayors. The vestigial sleeves of the sleeved variety can still be seen in academic dress.   *Ill. 86*

The clothes of the upper classes during the first half of the sixteenth century were extremely brightly coloured. We learn from the wardrobe inventories of Henry VIII that he possessed, among many others, doublets of blue and red velvet lined with cloth-of-gold. In 1535 Thomas Cromwell made his royal master a present of a purple velvet doublet embroidered in gold; and some of the King's garments were so heavily encrusted with diamonds, rubies and pearls that the underlying material was invisible.

Red was a favourite colour. In the well-known portrait of the Earl of Surrey, formerly attributed to Holbein, the young nobleman is shown completely clad in various shades of scarlet. In Cranach's portraits of German princes nearly all of them are wearing red, and, in spite of sumptuary laws, the middle classes imitated them as far as they dared. It is a curious comment on human aspiration that during the Peasants' Revolt in Germany, one of the demands of the insurgents was that they should be allowed to wear red clothes like their betters.

87 *Emperor Charles V with his dog*, by Titian, 1532

88 *Anne of Austria, Queen of Spain*, by Sanchez Coello, 1571. A further step in the development of the ruff

89 *A tailor*, by Giovanni Battista Moroni, *c.* 1571, an example of middle-class costume

90 *Portrait of a young man*, by Angelo Bronzino, *c.* 1540. The clothes of the upper classes show strong Spanish influence (*see also Ill. 91*)

And then, about the middle of the century, everything changed. The German domination of European fashion, with its bright colours and fantastic forms, gave way to Spanish modes, tight-fitting and sombre, preferably black. This was partly due to the personal taste of the Emperor Charles V, who was famous for the sobriety of his dress, and partly to the growing power of Spain. When in 1556 Philip II succeeded Charles V as King of Spain, the Spanish Court became the admired exemplar for all Europe. Even the French King Henry II followed the Spanish fashion and almost always wore black.

In England the tendency to wear more sombre colours can already be seen in the closing years of the reign of Henry VIII. The boy King Edward VI, who succeeded him, was unlikely to have much influence on fashion, and when he died and Mary Tudor ascended the throne, the trend was emphasized. Her

Ill. 87

91 *Pierre Quthe*, by François Clouet, 1562

marriage in 1554 to the Spanish King completed the revolution, for although the clothes of the Spanish courtiers who came to England in his train at first seemed strange to English eyes, the English soon adopted similar garments themselves. Even when *Ill. 93* Mary was succeeded by Elizabeth, even when England and Spain were at war, the Spanish influence persisted, and can be noted, with little modification, until the end of the century.

It was not only in colour, or the lack of it, that the new fashions differed from those of the preceding generation. There was a real difference in cut. Cunnington sums up the special features of the new mode as 'bombast, small waists and the introduction of knitting' (*Handbook of English Costume in the Sixteenth Century*). Bombast was the stuffing used in doublets and hose in order to swell them out, eliminating all folds and creases. It consisted of rags, flock, horsehair, cotton or even bran, although this last sometimes led to disaster, since all the bran ran out if the clothes got torn. The bombasting of the doublet over the chest and the stuffing out of breeches naturally made the waist seem smaller, and the effect was increased by the use of tight-lacing. The short, bombasted breeches, especially in the form of trunk hose, exposed a considerable expanse of leg, and the introduction of knitting made it possible for leg coverings to fit the limbs more neatly than they had done before.

The effect of all this was a new rigidity and *hauteur*, reflecting the stiff and proud etiquette of the Spanish Court. Gone were the easy flowing lines of the costume of the earlier part of the century, when clothes seemed to express a man's own person- ality, even his own fantasy. Instead men now seemed to be indicating their membership of an aristocratic caste. They hold themselves upright in padded and stiffened garments which form a veritable *cuirasse*. Art historians have noticed that Court portrait painting all over Europe represents its subjects standing, with one foot advanced, in an attitude of proud withdrawal, hieratic and stiff. And this effect was enhanced by the growth of the ruff.

92 *Mary I, Queen of England*, by Antonis Mor, 1554
93 *Queen Elizabeth I 'Rainbow Portrait'*, c. 1600

We have already noted the draw-string through the upper
edge of the shirt from which the ruff derived. It was only
necessary to draw the string tight round the neck and an
incipient ruff was already in being. When, as in the 1570s, it
appeared above the high-standing collar of the doublet, it held
the head high in an attitude of disdain. It goes without saying   *Ills. 94–5*
that the ruff was a mark of aristocratic privilege. It is an extreme
example of the tendency of men's clothes to show that their
wearers do not need to work, or indeed to engage in any
strenuous pursuit; and, as the century progressed, ruffs grew
larger and larger until it is difficult to see how their wearers
could have conveyed food to their mouths.

The ruff is an example of the 'hierarchical' element in dress.
Women wore it too, but in female dress there is always another
element to be noted. This – the 'Seduction Principle' as it has
been called – is an attempt to exploit the wearer's charms as a

91

94 *Magdalena, Duchess of Neuburg*, portrait formerly attributed to Peter Candid (de Witte), *c.* 1613. The elaborate triple ruff of the early seventeenth century.

95 *Queen Elizabeth at Blackfriars,* by Marcus Gheeraerts, *c.* 1600

woman, as, for example, by the use of décolletage. Women wished to wear a ruff in order to show their status in society: they also wished to be attractive as women. The 'Elizabethan compromise' was to open the ruff in front so as to expose the bosom, and to allow it to rise in gauze wings at the back of the head. This can be seen quite clearly in contemporary portraits of Queen Elizabeth.

Ills. 93, 95

The effect of the vertical line now dominant in costume was accentuated by the abandonment of flat caps (although apprentices were still compelled by law to wear them by an Act of Parliament of 1571) in favour of hats of various kinds. Some of the hats were in fact bonnets with a tall crown, which was sometimes stiffened with buckram; others were true hats made of stiff or stiffened materials. One of these was the so-called *copotain* which had a high conical crown; another

Ill. 98 variety resembled a modern bowler. They could be made of beaver, felt or leather, and could, if wished, be furnished with a plume and a jewel attached to the hat-band. There were also hats with broad brims and flat crowns, affected by magistrates and professional men. These were worn flat on the head: the Elizabethan gallant nearly always wore his hat at an angle or on the back of the head.

Women, too, began to wear hats in place of the hoods or bonnets with which they had been content for so long. At first they were used chiefly for riding or travelling. They were similar to men's hats but smaller and were often worn over a linen cap. But, as hairdressing became more elaborate, this coif was gradually discarded. The headdress usually hid the back hair, which was plaited behind the head, but the front hair was visible, and considerable variation in arrangement can be seen in contemporary portraits. Until the 1570s it was often fluffed out at the temples with a central parting. Then it was turned back over a pad, and finally raised over a wire support known as a 'palisadoe'. Queen Elizabeth set the fashion for dyeing the hair red, and many women, like herself, must have found it necessary to make use of false hair. In her old age the Queen wore a wig.

The rigidity which marked men's clothes in the second half of the sixteenth century was even more pronounced in those of women. The stomacher which formed the front of the bodice was stiffened with buckram or pasteboard and held in

96, 97 Opposite, three granddaughters and the son of Mildred, Lady Burghley, from her tomb in Westminster Abbey, 1589. The little girls' hair is enclosed in a kind of chignon. The advantage of sculpture is that it enables us to see the ruff from the back

98 Middle-class and servant's costume from *Description of England*, late sixteenth century

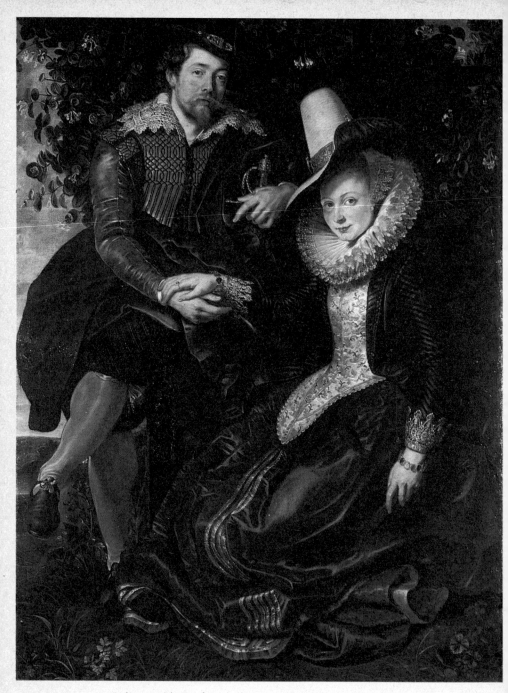

99 *Rubens and his wife Isabella Brant*, by Rubens, 1610. The painter wears the new falling collar, his wife the ruff. Her corsage is kept in place by a rigid busk

100 *Sigmund Feierabendt, the bibliophile*, by J. Sadeler, 1587. Costume of the middle-class scholar

place by busks, often of wood and therefore unbending. The skirt was swelled out by means of the farthingale. Its origin was universally acknowledged. It was the 'Spanish farthingale' or 'vertingale', and in its original form it consisted of an underskirt distended by hoops of wire, wood or whalebone, growing larger towards the bottom of the skirt. It therefore very closely resembled the nineteenth-century crinoline in its construction. It first appeared in England about the year 1545 and was soon worn by all women but those of the labouring classes.

The 'French farthingale', which came in about 1580, was more of a Court garment. It was called the 'wheel farthingale', which is a sufficient description of its general effect. It was as if the wearer were standing inside a wheel, with the skirt attached to the outer rim and falling vertically to the ground. In the well-known painting *Queen Elizabeth at Blackfriars*, the Queen and all her ladies are seen wearing this singularly unbecoming garment, which made women look as if they were hobby-horses. Rather similar was the 'Italian farthingale', made

Ill. 95

97

101 Ball at the Court of King Henry III of France, late sixteenth century

of wire or whalebone and worn slightly tilted at the back by means of a cushion, like a primitive bustle. The width could be as much as forty-eight inches.

A more popular fashion, outside Court circles, was the 'roll farthingale', vulgarly known as the 'bum roll'. This consisted of a padded roll of cloth in the shape of a polony, or boiling sausage, the two ends being joined together at the front of the body with tapes. By the end of the century it had become unfashionable, as is indicated by a character in Ben Jonson's *The Poetaster* who remarks that she has 'debased' herself from the farthingale to 'those bum rolls'.

In addition to the boned bodice and farthingale-extended skirt, women's principal garment at this period was the gown, which fell in folds from fitted shoulders, leaving a gap in the front through which the dress underneath could be seen. The sleeves were puffed, and ended above the elbow to reveal the

98

102 *Sir Christopher Hatton*, Anon., 1589   103 *Sir Walter Raleigh*, Anon., c. 1588

undersleeve. Sometimes long, vestigial, hanging sleeves were worn, attached to the upper sleeve. Other garments mentioned in contemporary inventories were the coat, a kind of loose jacket worn for warmth; the frock, which seems to have been a loose gown; and the cassock, which was of a similar form but with loose, open sleeves. For travelling, cloaks were worn and also a garment known as a 'safeguard', which seems to have been an over-skirt of plain material used both for warmth and to protect the rich stuff of the gown.

Men, too, began to employ a greater variety of garments. *Ills. 102–3* The doublet was still the main item in a gentleman's wardrobe, but over this could be worn the jerkin or jacket, often sleeveless. The cloak had now become indispensable, but it was no longer the long cloak of the preceding generation but a short cloak, sometimes hung from one shoulder. Although it had originally been a riding cloak, it was worn, during the second half of the sixteenth century, indoors as well as out. It was made of rich materials, and the really fashionable man required three cloaks, one for morning, one for afternoon and one for evening. Cloaks sometimes had standing collars, and were sometimes provided with a tippet, usually of velvet.

Men also wore the garment known as a 'cassock', which was a loose jacket reaching to the hips, and a gabardine which was a long, loose overcoat with wide sleeves. But the most curious item in the Elizabethan gentleman's wardrobe was the mandilion or mandeville. We cannot do better than quote Cunnington's description: 'Originally a military habit, it was a loose hip-length jacket with standing collar and hanging "coat" sleeves (later sham) and wings. The side seams were open, producing a front and back panel. It was buttoned from collar to chest only, and put on over the head. It was frequently worn "Collie-Westonward", or awry, "Collie Weston" being a Cheshire saying for anything that goes wrong. The garment

Ill. 103 was thus worn sideways, with the front and back panels draping the shoulders, while one sleeve hung down in front and the other behind' (*Handbook of English Costume in the Sixteenth Century*).

Male nether garments showed some peculiar variations in the second half of the century. Ordinary trunk hose could now

Ill. 95 be worn with 'canions'. These were breeches worn underneath the trunk hose (and often of a different material) and reaching to the knee. The stockings could be drawn over them, so that we might say that the 'hose' of the medieval period has now divided into three separate garments.

True breeches, if we may call them such, dispensed with trunk hose altogether. They could take various forms. 'Venetians' were rather baggy breeches fastening below the knee with buttons or points. They came in about 1570, but were most popular in the last twenty years of the century. When very baggy they were called 'galligaskins', 'gascoynes' or 'slops'.

With such garments stockings acquired a new importance. They were cut on the cross from cloth until about 1590, after

100

104 *Richard Sackville, Earl of Dorset*, by Isaac Oliver, 1616. He wears the transitional form between the ruff and the falling collar

which they were increasingly replaced by knitted stockings, sometimes of silk. They were sometimes of bright colours, yellow being a favourite, and were often adorned with clocks *Ill. 104* of coloured silk or even with gold thread, and were gartered in various ways: by a simple ribbon (which could, however, be adorned with gold thread or even with jewels) tied below *Ill. 95* the knee, the bow being at the side; or by cross-gartering, which did not in the least resemble what many Shakespearean producers imagine it to have been, i.e. a kind of trellis-work covering the entire leg. Cross-gartering, which was fashionable from 1560 onwards, was formed by a piece of ribbon encircling the leg below the knee, crossed at the back, brought forward above the knee and tied in a bow.

Footwear consisted of shoes or boots. The shoes were *Ill. 104* moderately rounded and were just beginning, as the century closed, to have heels. They could be made of leather, silk, velvet or plain cloth. The soles could be of leather or cork. Pumps and slippers were worn indoors. Boots, which until the last quarter of the century were used only for riding, became general wear, even indoors. The fashionable variety was close-fitting and reached to the thigh, the top being sometimes turned down in different ways. Such boots were only made possible by the improvements in leather-dressing originating in Cordoba. Our English word 'cordwainer' means a man who has derived his craft from this Spanish city.

Spain was also responsible for the fine leather gloves so much prized by the Elizabethans and which only began to be manufactured in England from about 1580. The most usual form was provided with gauntlets, which were often decorated with gold thread and fringed. They could also be perfumed, and were in general carried in the hand or tucked into the belt. The elegant gentleman also required a handkerchief, which was made of fine linen, embroidered or edged with lace. The clothes and accessories of the upper classes in Europe had indeed reached an astonishing degree of elaboration and refinement by the end of the sixteenth century.

CHAPTER FIVE

The seventeenth century

WE HAVE SEEN that during the second half of the sixteenth century Spain set the dominant tone in fashion. This influence persisted into the 1600s, but with certain modifications, notably in the abandonment of the stuffed and busked 'peascod' doublets and in the widening of the sleeves. The ruffs, too, became smaller in France and England, but continued to grow even larger in the Netherlands.

The doublet in the early years of the century had a short skirt consisting of a number of overlapping tabs, but from about 1610 these tabs were longer and curved down in front to a sharp point. The garment was provided with a high-standing collar buttoning in front, but generally concealed by the ruff. This was carried over from the preceding century but with certain variations, being sometimes in double or treble layers of tubular pleats starched by means of 'setting sticks'. Ruffs were usually white but sometimes yellow. The invention of starch, denounced by Puritan moralists as a new vanity, at least allowed the ruff to dispense with the wire frame or 'underpropper' which had previously been necessary.

In France, Henry IV, in contrast to Henry III, was a man of simple tastes. He was by no means a prude, being famous as *le Vert Galant* for his amours; but he had no liking for extravagance in dress, and issued several sumptuary laws, largely aimed at preventing the import of expensive materials of foreign manufacture. This had most effect on the dress of the *bourgeoisie*, members of which began to wear clothes made of wool. The courtiers continued to wear silk, but with fewer trimmings of gold and silver thread.

105–8 French noblemen and noblewoman, by Abraham Bosse, c. 1629–36. All the men have the characteristic 'bucket-top' boots of the period. *Ills. 106 and 107* show the development of the falling collar

Women's clothes, although still elaborate, were more natural, in that the female body was not so much deformed as it had been by tight-lacing and the cumbrous farthingale. Women benefited, too, by the transition from the ruff to the falling
Ill. 108 collar, and this tendency was even more apparent after the assassination of Henry IV and the accession of Louis XIII.

Fortunately we have a valuable documentation of the costume of this period in the engravings of Abraham Bosse. Scholars are agreed that they are not fanciful but give a faithful picture of the modes and manners of the time. From these engravings and from the etchings of Jacques Callot we can gain a very clear idea of the costume which in France is associated
Ills. 105–7, with *The Three Musketeers* and in England was the dress of the
109 'Cavaliers'. There was about it an element of martial swagger, with its breeches and doublet, its short cloak hanging from

104

109 *Gallery of the Palais Royal*, full of stalls selling every kind of finery. Engraving by Abraham Bosse, c. 1640

one shoulder, its wide-brimmed hat adorned with a plume and, above all, its boots. These could be of various forms, but the most characteristic style was that of the so-called 'funnel boots', with wide turnovers sometimes trimmed with lace. These were really riding boots, but from about 1610 they were frequently worn in town and indoors.

When shoes were worn, they were decorated with enormous rosettes, made of ribbons, lace and spangles and often extremely costly. Women's shoes were simpler, being almost completely concealed by the long skirt. In wet weather *chopines* were worn. These were wooden clogs covered with leather, worn under the shoes and sometimes with soles thick enough to qualify as stilts. They had been known since the beginning of the century (and in Venice from a much earlier date), as we can gather from Hamlet's remark: 'Your ladyship is nearer heaven than when I saw you last, by the altitude of a chopine.'

110 *Henry Rich, 1st Earl of Holland,* studio of Daniel Mytens, 1640. The new passion for lace, worn at the sitter's throat and, more inventively, in the tops of his boots

111 *Wedding celebration*, by Wolfgang Heimbren, 1637

Women's dress consisted of the bodice, the petticoat and the gown. The bodice was sometimes extravagantly décolleté and laced with a silk ribbon in front. The lacing was often covered with a 'piece' or 'plastron'. The sleeves were large, slashed or paned, and puffed out with stuffing. The character-istic skirt of the period was in fact two skirts, the over-skirt being gathered up to reveal the skirt underneath. The falling collar became ever more elaborate, with a border of costly lace.

Hair was generally worn rather flat on the top of the head, but frizzed out at the sides in thick curls. Women in general did not wear hats, but out of doors they provided themselves with little hoods of black taffeta or else wore a simple lace fichu on their heads.

What we have been describing were in effect French modes. In England they were copied, as we have noted, by the Cavaliers. The Puritans on the other hand, tended to derive their fashions (if such a frivolous word may be allowed in this connection) from Holland.

The system of government of the Protestant Netherlands was different from that obtaining elsewhere in Europe. Holland was ruled by a prosperous *bourgeoisie*, a body of influential and pious merchants and magistrates known as 'regents'. They wore a distinctive costume of conservative cut and black in hue. There is a paradox in this, for the Dutch had fought bitterly to obtain their freedom from Spain, and yet the formality and sobriety of their costume continued to show a Spanish influence. Indeed, it seemed to them suitable raiment for their own austere brand of Protestantism. But the most striking thing

112 Left, *Autumn*, after W. Hollar, *c.* 1650

113 The persistence of the ruff: *Portrait of a middle-aged woman with hands folded,* by Frans Hals, 1633

As Autumne fruit doth mourne and wast
And if not pluckt it droppe at last   Autumne   *So of herselfe (she feares) she shall*
If not timely gather'd fall.

about Dutch costume in the first half of the seventeenth century is the persistence of the ruff. It not only persisted; it grew larger and larger until it became a literal cartwheel of elaborately goffered linen folds, as can be seen in the portraits of Frans Hals. The English Puritans never copied this fashion. Many Dutchmen, however, wore their hair short, and this became the characteristic of the Parliament men in England: hence the nickname 'Roundheads'.

Ill. 113

We gain a charming glimpse of English fashions in the middle of the century from the engravings of Wenzel Hollar. Women wore their hair flat on the top of the head, with side curls or ringlets. The bodice was cut low, but with a linen kerchief or collar, which was sometimes transparent. The three-quarter-length sleeves had turn-ups of lace. The bodice came to a deep point and was laced down the front with visible ribbons. The skirt fell in folds to the ground. The general effect might be described as a stylish modesty.

Ill. 112

But the strange and, according to the moralists, immodest fashion had already arrived of wearing patches on the face. The satirist John Bulwer in his *Artificial Changeling*, published in 1653, ridicules the ladies' 'vain custom of spotting their faces out of an affectation of a mole, to set off their beauty, such as Venus had; and it is well if one patch will serve to make their faces remarkable, for some fill their visages full of them, varied into all manner of shapes'. Such shapes might be stars, crescents or even a coach and horses, cut out of black 'court plaster'. This strange fashion lasted for more than fifty years.

The Restoration of Charles II in 1660 brought with it the triumph of French modes, although significant differences continued to exist between the clothes worn in France and those worn in England. The fashions which Charles brought with him and which were adopted by his Court were among the strangest male garments ever worn. Subsequent historians have regarded them with an unfavourable eye. 'Taste and elegance', says F. W. Fairholt, 'were abandoned for extravagance and folly; and the male costume, which in the time of

Charles I had reached the highest point of picturesque splendour, degenerated and declined from this moment.' *(Costume in England,* 1885.)

Randle Holme, writing in 1684, described men's clothes as consisting of 'short-waisted doublets and petticoat breeches, the lining lower than the breeches, tied above the knee, ribbons up to pocket-holes half the length of the breeches, then ribbons all about the waistband, the shirt hanging out' *(Accidents of* *Ill. 114* *Armoury).* The petticoat breeches were a French fashion, or rather had become French, having been introduced by a certain Comte de Salm, known as 'the Rhinegrave'. The breeches were therefore called 'Rhinegraves' and were first worn in England, two years before the Restoration, by William Ravenscroft. They were then regarded as something of a curiosity, but after 1660 they became for a time universal among men with any pretension to fashion. They were so wide that, as Samuel Pepys tells us in an entry in his *Diary* for 1661, it was possible to put both legs into one compartment.

114 Suit with petticoat breeches, *c.* 1665

116 Sir Thomas Isham's wedding suit, *c.* 1681

The two suits show the transition from doublet with petticoat breeches to the 'vest' 'after the Persian mode', seen for the first time at Court in 1666

115 *Two ladies of the Lake family*, by Peter Lely, c. 1660

The extremely short doublet, so short that it showed a gap of shirt between its lower edge and the top of the breeches, was now buttoned down the front and resembled a sleeved waistcoat. There was a mania for bunches of ribbon, worn not only on the breeches but on the shoulders and elsewhere. We hear of a suit and cloak of satin, trimmed with thirty-six yards of silver ribbon, and no less than 250 yards of ribbon in bunches were used on one pair of petticoat breeches. The general effect of men's clothes at this period was of a fantastic negligence, well suited to the moral climate of the Restoration Court.

Ill. 115 Women's clothes were equally loose and apparently careless, so that most of the Court beauties painted by Lely seem to have been caught, as it were, in *négligé*, although some allowance must no doubt be made for the painter's poetic fancy. The style had its own attractiveness and even the sober Planché is moved to enthusiasm. 'A studied negligence,' he says, 'an elegant déshabille, is the prevailing character of the costume in which they are nearly all represented; their glossy ringlets escaping from a simple bandeau of pearls or adorned by a single rose, fall in graceful profusion upon many necks unveiled by even the transparent lawn of the band or the partlet; and the fair round arm, bare to the elbow, reclines upon the voluptuous satin petticoat while the gown of the same rich material piles up its voluminous train in the background.' (*A Cyclopaedia of Costume*, vol. II 1879, pl. 242.)

There was not much change in female dress during the greater part of Charles II's reign. The long pointed waists continued and gradually became tighter. The tucked-up skirts, known, confusingly, as *manteaux*, grew more formal in appearance, the general outline of the figure stiffer and narrower. The large collars of lace went out of fashion in the early 1670s, although, out of doors, a kerchief called a 'palatine' covered the bare shoulders. But while women's clothes remained comparatively static, those worn by men underwent a real revolution, the ultimate consequences of which can still be seen in modern dress.

117 *Charles II on horseback*, by Pieter Stevensz, *c.* 1670. The King is in the new fashion with lace *rabat*, full-bottomed wig and plumed hat anticipating the *tricorne*

It is strange that the name of Charles II, of all people, should *Ill. 117* be associated with a 'reform' of dress. Perhaps he was sobered for a moment by the plague and fire that had just devastated his capital, but, at all events, within little more than a month of the extinguishing of the fire, he took the step which provoked so much comment in contemporary diaries and memoirs. 'In this month', we read in Rugge's *Diurnal* for 11 October 1666, 'his Magestie and whole Court changed the fashion of their clothes, viz., a close coat of cloth pinkt, with a white taffety under the cutts. This in length reached the calf of the leg, and upon that a surcoat cutt at the breast which hung loose and shorter than the vest six inches. The breeches, the Spanish cut, and buskins some of cloth, some of leather, but of the same colour as the vest or garment.'

113

Pepys, too, describes the new dress and is even more precise in his dates. On 8 October 1666 he notes in his *Diary*: 'The King hath yesterday in Council declared his resolution of setting a fashion of clothes which he will never alter.' On 15 October he comments: 'This day the King begins to put on his vest, and I did see several persons of the House of Lords and Commons too, great courtiers, who are in it; being a long cassocke close to the body, of black cloth, and pinked with white silke under it, and a coat over it, and the legs ruffled with black riband like a pigeon's leg; and, upon the whole, I wish the King may keep it, for it is a very fine and handsome garment.'

Evelyn's *Diary* is equally explicit. Under the date 18 October, he remarks: 'To Court, it being the first time his Majesty put himself solemnly into the Eastern fashion of vest, changing doublet, stiff collar, bands and cloak, into a comely dress after the Persian mode, with girdles or straps, and shoestrings and garters into buckles, of which some were set with precious stones, resolving never to alter it, and to leave the French mode, which had hitherto obtained to our great expense and reproach. Upon which divers courtiers and gentlemen gave his Majesty gold by way of wager that he would not persist in this resolution.'

Charles, however, did persist – but he made certain modifications. Pepys notes (17 October 1666) that 'the Court is full of vests, only my Lord St Albans not pinked but plain black; and they say the King says the pinking upon white makes them look too much like magpies, and therefore hath bespoke one of plain velvet.' Evelyn described the new garment as a 'dress after the Persian mode', and as 'the Eastern fashion of vest'. Other contemporary references call the new fashion 'Turkish'; and one has to admit that it does bear a certain resemblance to the Persian coat except that the latter had long sleeves, whereas the sleeves of Charles's 'vest' were extremely short, the white shirt sleeve ballooning out below it.

Curiously enough the Persian coat was not entirely unknown

118 *Sir Robert Shirley*,
by Anthony van Dyck,
1622. Anticipation of the
fashionable clothes of half
a century later

at the English Court, Sir Robert Shirley having regularly worn *Ill. 118*
it as long before as the reign of Charles I. Shirley, who had
travelled much in Persia in the early years of the seventeenth
century, occupied the strange position, for an Englishman, of
Persian Ambassador at the Court of St James's. English relations
with Persia were, indeed, very close throughout the century;
and a new fillip to English interest in the East was given when
Charles II received the island of Bombay as part of the dowry
of Catherine of Braganza.

The English King's action was looked upon as a deliberate attempt to break away from French fashions, a step that was hardly likely to please Louis XIV, who was then endeavouring, with considerable success, to make France the arbiter of Europe, not only politically but also in matters of taste. Pepys notes (22 November 1666) that 'the King of France hath, in defiance to the King of England, caused all his footmen to be put into vests, and that the noblemen of France will do the like; which, if true, is the greatest indignity ever done by one prince to another'. French scholars, however, have pointed out that a very similar garment was introduced at the French Court as early as 1662. It was at first worn only by a few privileged courtiers, but by 1670 its use had become universal.

How did it come about that this Persian mode became the ancestor of modern costume? Richard Heath notes that 'over the vest a loose overcoat was worn; but, since all reference to it is omitted by Evelyn, and Pepys speaks of seeing the Court full of vests, it was evidently only intended for outdoor wear' ('Studies in English Costume I', *Magazine of Art*, vol. XI, 1887–8). It can be seen, worn as an overcoat, in a contemporary engraving of the funeral of General Monck in 1670. In the end the overcoat became the coat, and the vest became what was later, when it had grown much shorter, to be called the waistcoat. It is interesting to note that London bespoke tailors still refer to a waistcoat as a 'vest'.

Ills. 119, 120 At first it was extremely long, almost as long as the coat, coming nearly to the knees and buttoned all the way down, almost completely concealing the breeches. The coat was rather plain, embroidery being reserved for the inner garment, and the wide falling collar disappeared, since the coat made it inconvenient. Instead a cravat of lace or muslin was worn.

There has been considerable controversy about the origin of this item of apparel. The name seems to imply that it was derived from the neckwear of the Croats in the French service and that it was copied first by the French officers and then by the courtiers of Louis XIV. A fine-lace industry had been

119 *Duke of Burgundy*, by R. Bonnart, *c.* 1695

120 Viol player, by J. D. de Saint-Jean, 1695. The full-bottomed wig is now universal in polite society

established in France by the enlightened minister Colbert, and the King, anxious to encourage it, wore its products himself and decreed that nothing but *point de France* should be worn at Court. The well-known expert on old lace, Mrs Nevill Jackson, writing in *The Connoisseur*, remarks that 'the neckwear of a gentleman of fashion which immediately preceded the cravat was the rabat or falling collar, which in its turn had ousted the ruff, so that we are not surprised to find that the earliest cravats hang like the fronts of a turn-down collar, and are guiltless of bow or knot'.

117

121 Lady of Quality, by J. D. de Saint-Jean, 1693

122 Lady of Quality, *en déshabille*, by J. D. de Saint-Jean, 1687

Point de France, and the even more elaborate *point de Venise*, was extremely costly. We learn from the Great Wardrobe Accounts that Charles II paid £20. 12s. 0d. for a new cravat, and James II paid £30. 10s. 0d. for one to be worn at his own Coronation. These were very considerable sums in those days.

Towards the end of the seventeenth century the cravat had become narrower and longer. A bow of ribbon was sometimes worn behind it, and the cravat itself (no longer made of lace but of muslin or cambric) was sometimes knotted. At the Battle of Steinkirk in 1692 the French officers, summoned to repel a surprise attack, had no time to arrange their cravats properly. They accordingly twisted them quickly, drawing them through a buttonhole to keep them out of the way.

118

TOUT CE QUI RELUIT N'EST PAS OR

Mode d'imiter les gens de qualité
autant que faire se peut

Mode de trousser juppes et
manteau jusqu'aux épaules

Une belle
apparance
soutient le
credit

mode
d'être aussi braue. que Savoisine

Mode d'aller en pantoufle
par la ville

Mode de faire voir le bas de soye
Et la jarretiere à frange d'Or

123 *Mode bourgeoise*, by N. Guérard, *c.* 1690. The dress is remarkable for the profusion of lace with which it is trimmed. The high *fontange* is also of lace. The skirt is lifted to display the silk stockings

This was the origin of the 'steinkirk' which became a prevalent mode for about a dozen years not only in France but all over Europe.

We have noted that the old style of falling collar was inconvenient to wear with the new kind of 'vest'. It therefore shrank to a rabat; but another reason for its diminution in size was that the greater part of a falling collar would have been invisible anyway owing to the custom of wearing a periwig. In the preceding reign the prevailing fashion for long hair no doubt caused many gentlemen to provide themselves with *postiches*, but the effect aimed at was that of natural hair. By 1660, however, the periwig had become frankly artificial and it was adopted with such enthusiasm that no less than two hundred *perruquiers* were employed at the French Court.

The English Court took a little time to catch up, but by November 1663 Pepys was able to note in his *Diary*: 'I heard the Duke [of York] say that he was going to wear a periwig and they say the King also will. I never till this day observed

124, 125 Middle- and working-class costume, by S. le Clerc, end of seventeenth century that the King is mighty gray.' And in the entry for 15 February 1664 he remarks: 'To White Hall, to the Duke; where he first put on a periwig today: but methought his hair cut short in order thereto did look very pretty of itself, before he put on his periwig.' It was of course necessary to cut the hair close to the scalp, or even to shave it, to make the periwig fit.

In April 1664 he went to Hyde Park and 'saw the King with his periwig'. Pepys had already decided to adopt the new fashion, and one can't help feeling that he was a little disappointed at not making more of a sensation by wearing it when he went to church in it for the first time: 'I found that my coming in a periwig did not prove so strange as I was afraid it would for I thought that all the church would presently have set their eyes upon me.' The invaluable diarist tells us that in 1667 he paid £4. 10s. 0d. for two periwigs, and that a year later he arranged with his barber to keep his periwigs in good order for 20s. per annum. But of course the periwigs worn by the courtiers were much more expensive.

126, 127 Aristocratic costumes, by S. le Clerc, end of seventeenth century

The full-bottomed wig worn by men of fashion was extremely large and heavy, and active persons such as soldiers soon found it an encumbrance. We hear of a 'campaign' wig and a 'travelling' wig. The strange thing is that a wig of some kind was considered absolutely essential and that the fashion should have lasted, for the upper classes of Western Europe, for nearly a century.

Even more curious than the wearing of mountains of artificial hair was the use of powder. This certainly did not originate with Louis XIV, who disapproved of it and only adopted it when it had become a universal fashion at the end of his reign. The periwig of Charles II was black and remained so, and, from their portraits, it seems unlikely that either William III or Queen Anne ever wore powder. Indeed, powder does not come into general use until the 1690s. Pepys, whose *Diary* stops too soon, does not mention it at all. Evelyn, however, speaks of it in his *Mundus Muliebris*, published in 1694, but in this he was, of course, satirizing female fashions. The most definite evidence of the use of hair-powder by Englishmen is to be obtained from the dramatists of the period. Colley Cibber, in his famous comedy *Love's Last Shift* (1695) speaks of 'a cloud of powder beaten out of a beau's periwig'.

Women did not wear the periwig, but they aspired to the same lofty heights in their headdress by the invention of the *fontange*, so characteristic of the 1690s. It was named after one of the favourites of Louis XIV who, the story goes, finding her hair disarranged while hunting, tied it up hastily with one of her garters. The King expressed his admiration, and the mode was launched. Next day all the Court ladies appeared with their hair tied with a ribbon with the bow in front. The fashion quickly crossed the Channel and is one of the earliest examples of a French mode imposing itself on England, universally and almost at once.

Soon a simple bow of ribbon was not enough. Lace was added, and then a cap was added to the lace, with a wire frame to support the ever increasing height of the structure. It was

128 *James Stuart and his sister Louisa Maria Theresa*, by Largillière, 1695

then called, perhaps in irony, a 'commode', and in England was known also as a 'tower'. In the *Ladies Dictionary* of 1694 it is described as 'a frame of wire two or three stories high, fitted to the head, and covered with tiffany or other thin silks being now compleated into the whole headdress'. Moralists, as usual, regarded the new fashion with grave misgiving, as an incitement to pride, and Samuel Wesley the Elder, father of the more famous John Wesley, once preached a sermon against it, from the text: 'Let him that is upon the house-top not come down', drawing particular attention to the words 'Top-knot, come down.'

Various accounts are given of the derivation of the fashion and of the reasons for its disappearance. Louis XIV had grown tired of it by 1699 and expressed his disapproval, but it was the appearance at Court of an Englishwoman, Lady Sandwich, 'avec une petite coiffure basse', which really changed the mode. This must have been a personal eccentricity on the part of Lady Sandwich, for in general French fashions were dropped in England some time after they had been abandoned in France. We find the *Mercure Galant* for November 1699 remarking that the old style of high coiffure was beginning to appear ridiculous. Some ten years later Addison was commenting upon its final disappearance in England.

The male hat assumed, in the closing years of the seventeenth century, the shape it was to keep throughout the eighteenth. The hat of the Commonwealth, whether worn by Roundhead or by Cavalier (the latter wore it with a feather), was distinguished by its high crown and wide brim. Charles II brought in the so-called 'French hat', with wide brim and shallower crown, adorned with even more feathers than before. At the funeral of General Monck in 1670, already referred to, the hats are very small in brim also. Finally the crown settled down to a moderate height, and the brim, which had become wide again, underwent the process known as 'cocking' – that is to say, one portion of it was turned up either at the front, at the back or on one side of the head.

At first this seems to have been a matter of individual fancy: we hear, for instance, of the 'Monmouth cock'. In the reign of William and Mary the hat began to be turned up in three places, thus forming the 'three-cornered hat' which lasted for a century and was accepted as the only possible headgear for gentlemen throughout the civilized world. 'The cocked hat,' says Planché (*Cyclopaedia*, vol. I, 1876, p. 260), 'was considered as a mark of gentility, professional rank, and distinction from the lower orders who wore them uncocked.' Such differences as there were depended upon the width of the brim, the largest being known as the 'Kevenhuller'.

Hats, strangely enough, were worn indoors and even at dinner; it was only in the presence of Royalty that gentlemen went bare-headed. The hat and the periwig were symbolic of the extreme formality of manners that marked the closing years of the seventeenth century.

129 Wedding procession, from *Relazione del regno di Svezia* by Lorenzo Magalotti, 1674. The hat has begun to be cocked, but has not yet become the *tricorne*

130 *Madame de Pompadour*, by François Boucher, 1759

CHAPTER SIX

The eighteenth century

THE ESSENTIAL lines of eighteenth-century costume were, as we have noted in the previous chapter, already laid down in the last twenty years of the seventeenth. The enormous prestige of the Court of Versailles had already resulted, all over Europe, in a willingness to accept, in matters of fashion as in much else, the dominance of France. Henceforward fashionable clothes meant, for the upper classes at least, French clothes.

Versailles, however, was no longer the Court of a young King, avid for pleasure, but of an ageing monarch whose thoughts were turning to piety. Madame de la Vallière and Madame de Montespan had been replaced by the *dévote* Madame de Maintenon, and this change was reflected even in the courtiers' clothes. So far as materials were concerned, they were rich and splendid enough, but the easy, flowing lines of the earlier modes had given place to a new ideal of propriety and *tenue*. The general effect was of rigidity, dignity and seriousness. The new headdress for women – the *fontange*, which built up the hair into a peak crowned by a high cap – increased the apparent height and added to the vertical effect.

The same appearance of dignity was obtained by men, from 1680 onwards, by the *perruque à crinière* or full-bottomed wig. We have already dealt with the first appearance, at the Court of Louis XIV and the Court of Charles II, of the wig worn, not to conceal the lack of natural hair, but as an essential item in the dress of every upper-class man. It began to be powdered in the early years of the eighteenth century, and this strange custom persisted until the French Revolution.

The full-bottomed wig was an extremely cumbrous affair, and very expensive. It formed a mass of curls framing the face

131, 132 The full-bottomed wig of Lord Mohun, *c.* 1710 (right), has become in a generation the formalized wig of Martin Folkes, *c.* 1740 (left)

and falling below the shoulders. Fops wore it even longer. Until about 1710 it was also very high above the forehead. At home it was often replaced by an embroidered cap, and literary men and philosophers are sometimes shown in contemporary portraits as bare-headed but with their hair cropped close.

It was quite impracticable for any active pursuit, and soldiers soon evolved what was known as the 'campaign' wig. This continued to have a mass of curls but arranged in three locks of hair, one at the back and one at each side of the face, the ends being turned up and tied in a knot. The 'Ramillies wig' (called after Marlborough's victory over the French in 1706) was a further simplification. The hair was drawn back and tied in a long pigtail, generally with two bows of black ribbon, one at the top of the pigtail and a smaller one at the bottom.

133 *The five orders of periwigs,* by William Hogarth, 1761

On informal occasions men wore the bob wig, with the hair ending in a roll round the back of the neck. Clergymen and scholars affected a bob wig which was frizzed rather than curled. They also wore the 'tye' wig, with the hair drawn back into a queue tied with black ribbon. In the 'bag' wig this queue was enclosed in a square black bag or pouch, made of silk. The wig itself was sometimes black, but in general it was covered with white or grey powder. It could be made of human hair (this, naturally, being the most expensive) or of goat's hair, horsehair or vegetable fibres. Women, in general, did not wear wigs but powdered their own hair, sometimes added to by means of false curls worn at the back of the head.

The closing years of the reign of Louis XIV were marked by an increase, if that were possible, in stiffness and formality, but his death in 1715 opened a new era. As if in reaction against all that the Roi Soleil had stood for, women's clothes became looser and with more flowing lines. A contemporary notes in the magazine *La Bagatelle*, 1718, that 'at present comfort seems the only thing that the ladies of Paris care about when dressing'. *Ills. 134–6* The new form of dress was called a 'sack' or 'sacque', a comfortable, rather shapeless garment, with small box pleats behind. When these were double or treble and descended from the neck, merging below the shoulders into the folds of the gown, they were known as the 'sackback'. A more usual name is the 'Watteau pleat'. Scholars have attacked the term as erroneous, but it is certainly true that nearly all the ladies in Watteau's pictures are wearing it.

A curious feature of the clothes of this period was the return of hoops. Instead of height women now seemed to aim at width, and the skirt was distended sideways, sometimes to as much as fifteen feet, by means of whalebone or rods of osier. Hence the word *panier*, the French for 'basket', which the underlying structure of the skirt somewhat resembled. The extreme width of women's dresses at this period was the cause of some *Ill. 140* inconvenience, since it was impossible for two ladies to pass through a door side by side or even sit on the same couch. The

134, 135 The 'sack'. Left, *Lady Howard*, after Godfrey Kneller, *c.* 1710; right, *Mrs Anastasia Robinson*, after Vanderbank, *c.* 1723

fashion even had an effect on architecture, for example in the curved balusters of eighteenth-century staircases.

The classification of women's dresses at this period is a matter of some difficulty. Modern scholars have suggested a general division into 'open' robes and 'closed' robes, while acknowledging that such terms were never used at the time. The closed robe was a dress consisting of a bodice and petticoat (sometimes forming one garment) with no opening in the front of the skirt. The more characteristic open robe had a gap in the front of the skirt, in the shape of an inverted V, which allowed the petticoat to be seen beneath. This petticoat was sometimes quilted and sometimes embroidered even more lavishly than the skirt itself.

There was a similar arrangement of the bodice, which had a gap in front filled in by means of a stomacher shaped like a

131

shield and stiffened with pasteboard or busks. It was often heavily embroidered or decorated with a series of bows decreasing in size from top to bottom. The bodice was usually laced behind, and stiffened with whalebone.

The characteristic eighteenth-century sleeve ended just above or just below the elbow and was wide enough for the chemise-sleeve to emerge from it, with its ruffle of lace. Sometimes the ruffles were double or treble, the upper ones being slightly shorter so as to display the lace to better advantage. It was fashionable to match the lace on the ruffle with that on the cap and tucker. The latter was the white, frilled edging to the bodice, originally part of the shift but often sewn on separately. The 'modesty piece' had a similar function, that of concealing the lower part of the décolletage. The handkerchief, sometimes called a 'neckerchief', was a large square of linen, muslin or silk, folded and draped round the neck. (In fact, both terms are etymologically absurd, since the word 'kerchief', *couvre-chef*, originally meant a covering for the head.) There was also a

136 Sketches by Antoine Watteau

137 Costumes for a lady and her maid, from *La Couturière*, mid eighteenth century

138 Workroom of a dressmaker and diagrams to show the method of cutting, from the *Encyclopédie Méthodique*, 1748

version known as the 'half handkerchief', for informal occasions.

For three-quarters of the eighteenth century there was no essential change in the male mode established in the middle years of the reign of Louis XIV. Male dress consisted of coat, waistcoat and breeches. The coat was close-fitting to the waist and then flared out in skirts of varying length. It had three vents, one at the back and one at each side, the last two being pleated. The coat was either collarless or was provided with a narrow, upright band. There was a row of buttons down the front of the coat, but most of these were left unfastened. The

139 *The Graham children*, by William Hogarth, 1742. There is hardly any distinction between children's clothes and adult attire

140 *Mr and Mrs Andrews*, by Thomas Gainsborough, *c*. 1748. The gentleman is in informal country attire but the lady is wearing the extremely wide paniers of the current mode

sleeves were of great importance, and it is often possible to date clothes by the gradual diminution in the size of the cuffs as the century progressed. At first they were extremely large, being turned back and buttoned either just below or just above the elbow. Beneath the cuff showed the ruffle of the shirt, the lace used matching the lace of the shirt front.

Beneath the coat was the waistcoat, of different material and sometimes heavily embroidered. After the middle of the century the embroidery spread to the coat itself. In the early years of the century the waistcoat was almost as long as the coat and, like it, was furnished with buttons all the way down. The lower buttons were never fastened. It was close-fitting to the waist and then flared out in skirts with unpleated vents, often stiffened with buckram. The back of the waistcoat was made of less expensive material.

135

Knee-breeches were universally worn throughout the century. They were fairly loose and fitted over the hips without the need of either belt or braces. They were closed below the knee with three or four buttons, and at first the stockings were drawn over them. From about 1735, however, the breeches, closed with an ornamental buckle, were worn over the stockings.

Neckwear continued, without much variation, the tradition of the late seventeenth century, that is the cravat or the steinkirk described in the previous chapter; but from about 1740 younger men began to wear a stock, consisting of a piece of linen or cambric sometimes stiffened with pasteboard and buckled behind. Sometimes there was worn with it a black tie known as a 'solitaire'. This was usually worn with the bag wig.

141 *Two ladies sewing, c.* 1750

142 *Joseph Suss*, 1738

143 *Lady with straw hat*, by C. W. E. Dietrich, *c.* 1750

The three-cornered hat was almost universal throughout the
century, although country people and scholars sometimes wore
their hats uncocked. The usual practice was to turn up the brim
and attach it to the low crown in such a way as to form a triangle.
The brim was usually edged with braid, and a button or a jewel
was sometimes fixed to the left cock. The appearance of the
hat was naturally conditioned by the width of the brim. The
so-called 'Kevenhuller hat' had a wide brim, and was fashionable in the 1740s. The same is true of the Dettingen hat (called
after the Battle of Dettingen in 1743). It aimed at an effect of
military swagger. The usual colour of hats was black, although
Beau Nash, 'King of Bath', made himself deliberately conspicuous by wearing a white hat. The material was beaver, a
cheaper variety being made of rabbit fur.

137

144 *Thé à l'Anglaise chez la Princesse de Conti*, by Michel–Barthélemy Ollivier, 1766

145 *Girl with chocolate*, by Jean Etienne Liotard, mid eighteenth century. The girl's costume shows the characteristic time-lag at this period between servants' costume and that of their masters

By the 1760s we can begin to discern the tentative beginnings of a new style. In essence the change consisted of a decreasing emphasis on the French 'Court' style and an increasing adoption of English 'country' clothes. There was, in short, a trend towards practicality and simplicity. Coats were plain, had narrower cuffs and the skirts were sometimes cut away in front for ease on horseback. Even the universal three-cornered hat began to be replaced, at least for such pursuits as hunting, by a narrow-brimmed, high-crowned hat which served as a kind of primitive crash-helmet, and in which we can already see the outline of the top hat of the nineteenth century.

However, the 'macaronis' of the 1770s were a reaction against these developments. They wore very thin shoes with enormous buckles made of gold, silver, pinchbeck or steel and set with real or imitation stones. They affected very large buttons on their coats. Their hats were extremely small, but their wigs were dressed high on the head, prodigiously curled.

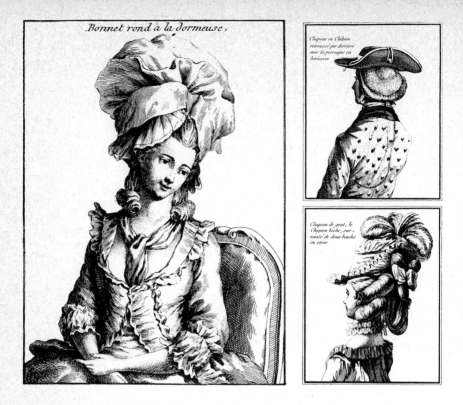

Bonnet rond à la dormeuse.

Chapeau en Clabaan retroussé par derrière avec la perruque en herisson

Chignon de goût, le Chignon lache, sur-monté de deux boucles en cœur

Ills. 148–
51 This was in line with the development of women's hairdressing at this period. The hair, having been dressed close to
the head since the age of the *fontange*, began to rise in the 1760s,
and we hear that 'Lady Strathmore's dress is the wonder of
the town, her head a yard high and filled, or rather covered
with feathers to an enormous size' (Letters of the Hon. Mrs
Osborn, 1767). This was probably an exaggeration in the
1760s, but became true in the 1770s. George Colman the
Younger describes a contemporary headdress: 'A towering
toupee pulled up all but by the roots and strained over a cushion
on the top of her head, formed the centre of the building;
tiers of curls served for the wings; a hanging chignon behind
defended her occiput like a buttress; and the whole fabric was
kept tight and water proof by a quantity of long single and
double black pins' (*Random Records*, 1770).

146 Far left, mob cap, 1780

147, 148 Male and female coiffures, *c.* 1778

149–152 Three female headdresses and man in a soft hat, *c.* 1778.

It was at this period that the headdresses of women reached their most exaggerated height. Men, on the other hand, were adopting a more simple style, even discarding the *tricorne*

The 'double pins' mentioned were what we would call hairpins, which came into use just about this time. The 'cushion' was a pad stuffed with tow, wool or horsehair, and because it induced headaches, it was later replaced by a wire frame over which the natural hair was draped, with false hair added. The whole was plastered with pomatum and covered with white powder. Such a structure, which sometimes remained untouched for months, soon became the resort of vermin, and the little ivory claws on the end of a long stick which antique dealers still refer to as 'back scratchers' were really made to insert into the headdress in an endeavour to relieve the intolerable itching.

The headdress was sometimes crowned with the most fantastic objects: a ship in full sail, a windmill with farm animals grouped about it, a garden with real or artificial flowers. Or

153 *The Morning Walk*, by Thomas Gainsborough, 1785

154 *Joseph II meets Catherine the Great*, by J. H. Löschenkohl, 1787

else a hat could be worn. Such hats were rather small in the early 1770s, but gradually grew larger. Some were of soft material, some with stiff crowns and wide brims adorned with feathers, as can be seen in Gainsborough's famous picture, *The Morning Walk*. This was painted in 1785, by which time the hair was being dressed broad instead of high, was frizzed instead of curled and was sometimes enclosed in an enormous mob cap instead of a hat. *Ill. 153*

Beginning in the 1770's, there was a marked change in the general outline of women's dress, which can be summed up as a transition from hoops to a kind of bustle. The bodice also began to be puffed out, giving a pouter-pigeon effect. Bodices were in general deeply décolleté, the gap being filled in with a neckerchief. Many women adopted a masculine style of

155 *N'ayez pas peur, ma bonne amie*, after Moreau le Jeune, *c.* 1776. A visit to the mother-to-be. The gentleman is an abbé. The visiting ladies are wearing the elaborate day clothes and the high headdresses of the period

156 *Les Adieux*, after Moreau le Jeune, *c.* 1777. The lady is entering a box at the Opera in full evening dress with enormous paniers and deep square décolletage

waistcoat, and even a 'great-coat' dress or 'riding-coat' dress with revers and a triple falling collar. Considerable variation in female attire was now possible, as we can see from *La Gallerie des Modes*, a pioneer in the field of the fashion plate, published in parts at irregular intervals between 1778 and 1787.

The fashion plate, indeed, sprang into existence at this period, with immense consequences in the dissemination of fashion. As Vyvyan Holland has pointed out in *Hand-coloured Fashion Plates, 1770–1899*, it is important to distinguish the fashion plate from the 'costume plate'. The latter attempts to show clothes 'after the event', as it were, as Wenceslas Hollar did,

157 *Le Rendez-vous pour Marly*, after Moreau le Jeune, *c.* 1776.
Walking dress of considerable elaboration

for example, in his *Ornatus Muliebris Anglicanus*, published in
1640, or as Jean Dieu de Saint-Jean did in France in his admirable
engravings of male and female costume at the Court of Louis
XIV. Even *Le Monument du Costume* of Freudenberg and
Moreau le Jeune, published in Paris between 1775 and 1783,
consisted of 'costume plates'.

Curiously enough the first true fashion plates were not
French but English. *The Lady's Magazine* was publishing them

158 *The Promenade at Carlisle House*,
by J. R. Smith, 1781. At this house of
assignation the gentlemen wear their
hats, the one on the left having
abandoned the *tricorne* and adopted
'country' clothes

159 *Coiffure sans redoute, c.* 1785. The
headdress, wide instead of high, is very
typical of the 1780s. On top is perched
the early form of the top hat. It is a
sign of female emancipation when
women start wearing hats

from 1770 onwards. And suddenly similar plates were being
published all over Europe. Accustomed as we are today to
fashion illustrations, it is hard for us to realize that, before the
invention of the fashion plate, information concerning the
latest fashion was so hard to come by that Marie-Antoinette's
dressmaker found it worth while to travel the Continent every
year in a huge *berline* containing dolls dressed in the latest
modes de Paris.

It would be very instructive for the student of costume to compare two sets of fashion plates, such as those in *La Gallerie des Modes* and those of Heideloff's *Gallery of Fashion* (he would have to do so in some great public library such as that of the Victoria and Albert Museum). Although a gap of a mere ten years separates these two publications, the clothes depicted in them are entirely different. What had happened in the meantime, of course, was the French Revolution.

Like all great social upheavals, this had a profound effect on the clothes of both men and women. The dress of the Ancien Régime was swept away. Suddenly there were no more embroidered coats or brocaded gowns, no more wigs or powdered hair, no more elaborate headdresses, no more *talons rouges*. 'Return to Nature' was the cry, but in the matter of costume this is never quite possible, unless people are willing to adopt the nudity of the savage. What, then, actually happened?

Ills. 160–63

160, 161 The newly invented fashion plate: *Gallerie des Modes, c.* 1778. Left, *Robe à la Polonaise*; right, dressmaker setting out to visit a client and carrying a pair of paniers

In male dress the quest for simplicity meant the abandonment of French 'Court' clothes and the acceptance of English country clothes. For a variety of historical reasons the English upper classes had never been content to flutter round a Court, like their French counterparts. They preferred to spend their time on their country estates. And for active pursuits such as fox-hunting they soon found that they were compelled to adopt a simpler form of dress from that considered fashionable in the capitals of Europe. They took all the embroidery off their coats and had them made of plain cloth. They abolished the lace ruffles at wrist and throat, put aside the white silk stockings and fitted their legs into stout boots. And, as we have already noted, for the universal three-cornered hat they substituted a primitive form of 'topper'.

Now, even before the French Revolution, there was much enthusiasm, even in France, for all things English. England was looked upon as a land of liberty (which indeed, by comparison,

162, 163 Walking and summer dresses, from Heideloff's *Gallery of Fashion*, 1795. Heideloff, a Swiss, was driven out of France by the Revolution and published his great work in England

Fig. 99.   *Fig. 100.*

164 Day dresses, 1796. Fashion plate from Heideloff's *Gallery of Fashion*. Plumes were worn in the hair even when walking in the country

165 *Point de Convention*, by Louis-Léopold Boilly, *c.* 1801. Even Frenchmen have now adopted English 'country' clothes

it was), and the result was a wave of anglomania which found its full expression when the privileges of the French nobility had been swept away. During the Terror, of course, it was dangerous to wear fashionable clothes of any kind, but after the execution of Robespierre, those who had survived the guillotine began once more to dress as they pleased. And what they were pleased to wear was a fantasticated version of English country clothes. The Englishman's hunting coat was given   *Ill. 165* tails of extravagant length, boots of extraordinary shapes replaced shoes, waistcoats became extremely short, collars rose to a great height behind the head, and neckcloths became so voluminous that they sometimes rose over the chin and even

166, 167 Morning dress of 1799 and ball dress of 1800

concealed the mouth. Wigs were abandoned, and the un-
powdered hair was worn in a wild mop sometimes brushed
forward over the forehead. Few more bizarre silhouettes have
ever been seen than those of the French *Incroyables* of the 1790s.

Women's dress at this period was less extravagant, but
showed an even more drastic break with the past. Paniers,
bustles and corsets were all abandoned, as were also the rich
materials of which dresses had formerly been made. Instead
women wore a *robe en chemise*, which did indeed look like an
undergarment, for it consisted of a white, high-waisted muslin
cambric or calico garment falling to the feet and sometimes so
transparent that it was necessary to wear white, or pink, tights
underneath. Sometimes the material was dampened so that it
clung to the body in imitation of the folds of the Greek dresses
represented in antique statues. Heelless slippers contributed to
this effect. Hairdressing was simplified with a similar intention,

but the effect was somewhat spoilt by the plumes of ostrich feathers which it was fashionable to stick in the hair. These were worn even in the daytime, but it should be emphasized that there was at this period very little difference between 'full dress' and 'morning dress' except in the quality of the materials. One curious result of the extreme flimsiness of women's clothes at this time was that pockets in the garments themselves became impracticable. Hence the appearance of a little handbag known as the 'reticule', or 'ridicule', which women began to carry about with them everywhere they went.

In France the accession of Napoleon to power put an end to the extravagance of male fashion under the Directoire. Englishmen had never adopted these strange modes, and by 1800 had settled down to a tightened and smartened version of country clothes: a top hat, a not too exaggerated neckcloth, a coat with revers and a collar of medium height, made of plain cloth and cut away in the front, a waistcoat, not as short as it had been in the 1790s, breeches with a square flap and diagonal side-pockets, and breeches fitting into riding boots. In the evening, pumps, knee-breeches and silk stockings were worn, and a *bicorne* was carried under the arm. The English had been slower than the French to abandon hair-powder, but when the Government imposed a tax on it in 1795, it ceased to be worn except by some of the older men. The pig-tail was given up except by the military, who kept it for another ten years.

In fact, by the end of the eighteenth century the general lines of costume were already laid down: for women a version of what came to be known as the 'Empire' gown; for men a costume which we can already recognize as that of 'John Bull'. These two modes, male and female, showed very little variation all over Europe. One is struck again by the fact that, since the seventeenth century, West European culture has been basically one, and that therefore there is little differentiation in the costume of the various nations, so far, at least, as the upper classes are concerned.

CHAPTER SEVEN

From 1800 to 1850

PERHAPS at no period between primitive times and the 1920s had women worn so little as they wore in the early years of the nineteenth century. All female attire seemed to have been designed for tropical climates, and yet the climate of Europe can have been no different in 1800 from what it was in 1850, when women wore ten times as many clothes. In France and England, the leaders in fashion, the accepted garb was a kind of light nightdress reaching, it is true, to the ankles but extremely décolleté even in the daytime. Ruffs came into the mode again, and there was a passion for shawls. Such shawls came *Ill. 172* originally from Cashmere, but the war with England made it difficult for the French to import them, and they therefore began to manufacture similar shawls of their own. Great Britain, too, began to produce imitation Cashmere shawls at Paisley. It was considered the mark of the fashionable lady to be able to wear a shawl with grace, and it formed an essential part of every woman's wardrobe.

168 Left, *Madame Récamier*, by François Gérard, 1802

169 *I have not learned my book, Mamma*, by Adam Buck, *c.* 1800

Napoleon's expedition to Egypt had induced in his compatriots a new wave of Orientalism which made turbans fashionable, and these were worn in England as well. Otherwise the outline aimed at a 'classical' effect, with the emphasis on vertical line; but the Oriental influences contributed to modify this ideal, and the classical style only lasted from about 1800 to 1803. An Egyptian influence could be noted for the next three years, and then, owing to the Peninsular War and interest in all things Spanish, gave way to Spanish styles, Spanish ornamentation being superimposed on what was still thought of as a classical garment.

In 1802 there was a cessation of hostilities between England and France, but the Peace of Amiens was short-lived, and for the next twelve years England and France were cut off from one another. When the English ladies flocked over to Paris in 1814 after Napoleon's first abdication, they found to their astonishment that English and French fashions had notably diverged. The French ladies were still wearing white, but the

170 *La belle Zélie,*
by J.-A.-D. Ingres, 1806

171 English outdoor dress,
c. 1807–10

172 Male and female walking dress, 1810

173 Summer walking dresses, 1817

Soon after Waterloo, French dresses ceased to be severely 'classical' and, with their heavy flouncing, foreshadowed the style to come

skirt, instead of falling straight to the ankles, now flared out slightly at the hem. English costume, on the other hand, was beginning to look 'romantic', with echoes of such Elizabethan elements as puffed and slashed sleeves. The result of this confrontation was that the English ladies immediately abandoned their insular fashions and adopted French modes.

The exact opposite happened in the case of men's dress. As we have seen, the English influence on male costume was already marked at the end of the eighteenth century, but now

157

174 *Thomas Bewick*, after James Ramsay, *c*. 1810. He wears the cutaway coat and top hat of English country costume, but still has knee-breeches

175 *Captain Barclay*, '*the celebrated pedestrian*', *c*. 1820. Trousers have replaced knee-breeches

176 Male and female walking dress. Fashion plate, 1818

Frenchmen plainly accepted English dress as the law. This was due in no small degree to the superior skill of London tailors. These had been trained to work in cloth, and cloth, unlike light silk and other flimsy materials, can be stretched and moulded to the body. The clothes of the eighteenth-century aristocrat were in general very badly made and did not fit at all snugly to the body. Such snug fitting was the very essence of dandyism, and George Brummell prided himself on the fact that his clothes did not show a single wrinkle and that his breeches fitted his legs like a natural skin. Dandyism does not imply gorgeousness in male attire; the exact opposite is the case. There was no embroidery on the dandy's coat: it was made of plain cloth, with the cut-away originally derived from the

158

177 Kensington Garden dresses for June, from *Le Beau Monde*, 1808. An early example of trousers

KENSINGTON GARDEN DRESSES for June
Engraved exclusively for Le Beau Monde or Library & Fashionable Magazine

hunting coat, and with a preference for the primary colours. Brummell's coat was invariably dark blue, but it was usual to wear waistcoat and breeches of a different colour; for example, a crimson waistcoat and yellow breeches could be worn with a blue coat, or a white waistcoat and sage-green breeches with a black coat. The collar, which stood rather high at the back of the neck, was sometimes of velvet. Waistcoats were in general short and square-cut, with perhaps a couple of inches showing below the front parts of the coat. The upper buttons were left undone to display the frill of the shirt. In Court dress the waistcoat was of white satin embroidered with gold thread.

In the daytime it was usual to wear tight-fitting breeches fitted into riding boots, but in the evening silk stockings were worn with pumps. Some men wore pantaloons or tights with tasselled hessians. Trousers were also worn, but, although close-fitting, did not show the shape of the leg and ended above the ankles. Very wide trousers *à la Turque* were also worn, with an anticipation of the wide trousers which were later to be called 'Cossacks'.

The dandy was shown not only by the cut of his clothes and the snugness of his breeches but by the elaboration of his neckwear. The collar of the shirt was worn upright; the two points projected on to the cheeks and were kept in place by a neckcloth, either in the form of a cravat or a stock. Some dandies were alleged to spend a whole morning in the arrangement of their cravats. Large squares of lawn, muslin or silk, folded cornerwise into a band, were wrapped round the neck and tied in a knot or bow in front. There is the well-known story of a caller visiting Brummell in the middle of the morning and finding his valet arranging his cravat. On the floor was a large heap of discarded cravats, and when the visitor inquired what they were, the valet replied, 'Sir, those are our failures.' The stock was a made-up, stiffened neckband, buckled behind. Since the wearing of either a cravat or a stock made it difficult, if not impossible, to turn or lower the head, it contributed in no small degree to the dandy's imperturbability and hauteur.

178 *Monstrosities of 1822*, by George Cruikshank. Example of exaggerated 'dandy' modes seen in Hyde Park near the statue of Achilles

Top hats of some form were worn at all times of day, but the correct hat for evening was the *bicorne*, in the shape of a crescent, the two brims being pressed against one another, which enabled the hat to be carried under the arm. Hair was short, and it was the fashion to wear it somewhat dishevelled *à la Titus*. Most civilians were clean-shaven, but side-whiskers and occasionally moustaches were worn by military men. The wearing of swords had been entirely abandoned, but it was fashionable to carry a cane; indeed, no well-dressed man was ever seen in the street without one.

Brummell's dress had always been of stolid sobriety, but after his departure in 1819 (he fled to the Continent to escape his creditors) the clothes of the dandies, or those who thought themselves such, began to develop all kinds of extravagances.

179 Walking dress, 1819   180 Carriage dress, 1824

The top hat swelled out at the top until its crown was wider than the brim, the visible ends of the shirt collar came up almost to the eyes, the stock or cravat grew tighter and higher, the shoulders of the coat were padded and the waist nipped in with the aid of a corset. Trousers had now become almost universal, either ending just above the half-boots or strapped under the instep. The caricaturists made merry with this new

Ill. 178 mode, for example in Cruikshank's *Monstrosities of 1822*.

The same year was a turning-point in female dress. The waist, which had been high for a quarter of a century, now resumed its normal position, and when this happens it inevitably becomes tighter and tighter. As a result, the corset once more became an essential element of female dress, even for small girls. A contemporary advertisement advises a mother to make her daughter lie face down on the floor in order that she might

162

181 French and German costumes, 1826   182 Evening and morning dress, 1831

then place a foot in the small of the back to obtain the necessary
purchase on the laces.

The effect of tight-lacing can be increased by widening the
skirt and puffing out the sleeves. Both of these were done in
the 1820s. Early in the decade the skirts were still fairly narrow,
but they were weighted at the bottom by a flounce, frills and
other decorations, sometimes even by a band of fur. The sleeves
were also modified, first by a little puff at the shoulders, which   *Ill. 181*
was imagined to be a harking back to the dresses of the
Renaissance. The Romantic movement was by now in full
swing, the novels of Walter Scott found innumerable readers
and every young woman seems to have wanted to look like
Amy Robsart or another of his heroines. There was even a
vogue for dresses made of Scotch plaid. About 1825 the little
puffed sleeve was provided with another sleeve over it, usually

163

183 Male and female riding costume, 1831. The *equestrienne* has masculin-
ized the *upper* half of her costume, but wears a long, trailing skirt

184 Dresses. Fashion plate, 1829

of transparent gauze. When this was made opaque, the sleeve
assumed the curious leg-of-mutton shape so characteristic of
the period. After 1830 the skirt was shorter, but even wider
than before, and the sleeves became enormous.

So did hats. The day cap worn in the home was much
expanded and no longer tied under the chin. Turbans became
extremely wide, so that they no longer looked like turbans but
became veritable hats. The hats themselves were extremely
wide in the brim. Though usually made of straw, they were also
of silk and satin and were trimmed with a mass of flowers,
ribbons and feathers in striking colours. From 1827 onwards
such hats were worn even in the evening at the theatre, making
it almost impossible for anyone sitting behind them to see the
stage. The diarist Croker complains that even at the dinner

185 Pelisse robe, silk brocade, 1831–3. The little puffed sleeve of the late 1820s has become the 'leg of mutton' sleeve of the early 1830s

186 Gentlemen's morning dress, 1834

table the size of the hats of his two companions prevented him from seeing his own plate. Caricaturists of the period delighted to show hats so huge that they served as umbrellas, not only for the wearer but for two companions walking by her side.

Hair was most elaborately arranged, with curls over the forehead and a chignon at the back of the head. Artificial hair was sometimes added in the evening in the form of what was known as the 'Apollo knot', fixed on the top of the head and decorated with flowers, feathers or combs. Some of these were of tortoiseshell set with jewels. Another possible addition was the 'Swiss bodkin', a long hat-pin with a detachable metallic head, derived, it would seem, from the peasant costumes of Switzerland.

After about 1828 skirts became slightly shorter, but sleeves continued to expand. The bodice gave an impression of width.

187 *In the garden*. Fashion plate, 1840. The modest little poke bonnet has replaced the elaborate hats of the previous decade

In the evening it was décolleté, sometimes extremely so, with a straight-across top edge to the corsage. In the daytime it was fashionable to wear a ruff, once more an imitation of what was imagined to have been the Elizabethan mode. A wide, flat collar called a 'pelerine' covered the shoulders. This was sometimes provided with hanging ends and was then known as a 'fichu-pelerine'. Out of doors in the daytime women wore a pelisse with enormous sleeves and many capes. With evening dress went various kinds of mantle. Shawls were still worn, but were less fashionable than they had been in the previous decade. In spite of the increased fullness of the skirt, reticules were still carried; muffs were fashionable throughout the decade, although they became somewhat smaller towards its close. A fan was an essential part of the evening toilette, and a

188 *Florence Nightingale and her sister Parthenope*, by W. White, *c.* 1836. The balloon sleeves, which have now slipped off the shoulder, are about to vanish altogether

large bouquet was often carried as well. The parasol was another essential part of the fashionable lady's equipment, but it was rarely put up because it would have had to be of enormous size to protect the hat. Instead it was carried in the hand. A great deal of jewellery was worn in the form of lockets, crosses, gold bracelets, mosaic and cameo brooches and gold chains supporting little bottles of perfume.

In 1837 the romantic, flamboyant modes of the first part of the decade began to be modified. Sleeves were no longer so wide, and the bulge had begun to slip down the arm. Skirts were longer again and did not show a woman's ankles when she walked. The boned corsage fitted closely to the body and was adorned in the front with a fan-shaped piece of material. The most striking change was in headgear: tied firmly under the chin, it was no longer a hat but a bonnet. It was worn close to the head in the form of a coal-scuttle and gave an impression of extreme modesty. By comparison with the fashions of the 1830s, indeed, the fashions of the 1840s became positively mouselike. Bright colours gave way to dark greens and browns. Shawls returned to favour. Elaborate hairdressing was abandoned except for the ringlets which framed the face.

Men's clothes, too, became more sombre at this period. Pinched-in waists and padded shoulders were abandoned as well as the flamboyant waistcoats and the dangling seals. The cut-away coat was still worn both in the evening and in the daytime, but in the evening it was now usually black. Many younger men began to prefer the frock coat in the daytime, and in summer the jacket, which had shorter skirts. Frilled shirts vanished from day wear, although they were for a time still fashionable in the evening. The cravat was smaller, although it still kept the shirt collar against the cheek. Sometimes the collar was almost entirely concealed by it. Sportsmen affected spotted neckcloths, kept in place with a pin. The top hat was universally worn by all ranks of society. Its crown was very high at the beginning of the decade, but grew smaller towards its close. In the country a low-crowned informal hat called a

168

'wide-awake' was sometimes worn. Nether garments consisted of trousers, rather tight and strapped under the instep. An alternative was pantaloons, which were tighter still and also strapped under the foot. Breeches were worn in the country, in which case they were made of leather or cord, and also at Court, where they were made of white cassinère. It was unusual for trousers to be made of the same material as coats. Scotch plaids were popular in winter, white drill trousers in summer.

Overcoats of the period show a surprising number of varieties: the top coat, the chesterfield, which was slightly waisted, and the paletot, which was a short coat and could take the place of the overcoat on occasion. The curricle, which was used for driving, had one or several pleats over the shoulders. Cloaks were worn over evening dress. The overcoats worn in France and Germany were essentially English in origin.

The anonymous author of a book on etiquette entitled *The Habits of Good Society*, published in the 1840s, tells us that the well-dressed man needed four kinds of coat: a morning coat, a frock coat, a dress coat and an overcoat. He needed four of the first and one each of the others, the cost of the seven coats being £18 (i.e. little more than £2 each). In addition he needed six pairs of morning and one of evening trousers, at a total cost of £9; and four morning waistcoats and one evening waistcoat, costing £4 in all. Another £10 was to be allowed for gloves, linen, hats, scarves and neckties, and £5 for boots. The well-dressed man of moderate means could therefore fit himself out for under £50 a year, which by modern standards seems extremely little. Of course the dandies, who still persisted into the 1840s, spent very much more than this. They were regarded as relics of a former, dissipated age. The dominant figure in English life was now a respectable bourgeois, who had no desire to make himself conspicuous but wished merely to present a gentlemanly appearance, both in his counting-house and at home. The author we have already quoted recommends dark blue or black for town wear, although he allows a tweed suit to be worn in the country. What we are watching, in fact, in this period is the fading away of flamboyance and colour from men's garments, not to be recovered until very modern times. It was considered ungentlemanly to wear anything striking.

Ill. 190   The same was true of women; quietness and delicacy were the qualities most admired. Indeed, it was fashionable to be, or to appear, a little *souffrante*; 'rude health' was positively vulgar. Rouge was entirely abandoned, 'interesting pallor' was admired, and some foolish young women even went so far as to drink vinegar in order to conform to the prevailing fashion. The prosperous businessman, who had now begun to desert the city and to establish his family in a fine new house in the fashionable suburbs, asked two things of his wife: first that she should be a model of domestic virtues, and second that she should not do anything at all. Her complete idleness was the mark of his social status. Work of any kind was looked down on, and the clothes which reflected this attitude were of an

190 *Convalescence*, after
Eugène Lami, *c.* 1845

191 Day dresses, from *Le Follet*,
c. 1848. Examples of the extremely
modest styles of the 1840s. The
Queen's passion for Balmoral
encouraged the use of Scotch
plaids

extremely restrictive kind. Indeed, the large number of petti-coats worn at this period prevented women from pursuing any activities without fatigue.

This seems all the more strange when we consider that in the world outside the home the 1840s was a decade of quite extraordinary innovation and upheaval. It saw the introduction of railways; it also witnessed a series of social upheavals cul-minating in 1848, the Year of Revolutions. In all this, women were supposed to have no part, and the vast majority of women seem to have accepted this situation with meekness and resig-nation. Prudery reigned supreme; skirts were now down to the ground, and the little feet in flat-heeled slippers could barely be glimpsed beneath the underskirts. As sensible a writer as Thackeray thinks it necessary to apologize for mentioning ankles. There never was a period when women, with the exception of the straight-across décolleté in the evening, were more completely covered up. The poke bonnet prevented even their faces from being seen except from directly in front.

Such a state of affairs did not, naturally, suit all women, and, in France at least, there was a wave of rebellion, symbolized by the figure of the *lionne*. A contemporary writer defines the *lionne* as a 'rich married woman, pretty and coquettish, who can handle the whip and the pistol as well as her husband, ride like a lancer, smoke like a dragoon, and drink any quantity of iced champagne'. 'Ride like a lancer' is the operative phrase. There was a passion for horsemanship among women in the early 1840s, and all fashionable magazines of the period show riding costume. The curious point about it is that it is masculin-ized down to the waist but no further. The practical thing, of course, would have been to masculinize the nether limbs; but it was unthinkable at this period that women should wear bifurcated garments, and they always rode side-saddle. Work-ing from the head to the feet, we may note that the correct female riding habit consisted of a man's top hat with a veil rather loosely attached to it, a man's collar and tie, a man's coat and waistcoat and an extremely voluminous skirt. In fact the

172

192 Winter dress, 1847

skirt was so voluminous that it reached almost to the ground when the wearer was in the saddle (as can be seen quite plainly in the equestrian statues of Queen Victoria at this period) and made it almost impossible to alight from the horse without help from a groom. The unconscious motivation is plain enough. One of the purposes of dress is (or perhaps we should say was) to show that the wearer is of high social status and can afford to employ a retinue of servants.

The essential lines of female costume during the 1840s may be briefly summarized. The waist was low, and the lines of decoration on the bodice were designed to make it look even more so. The sleeves were either tight or had a bulge over the lower arm; the skirts were long and full. Bodice and skirt were usually made in one, with a back fastening by means of hooks and eyes, but from the middle of the decade it was possible to have a jacket bodice separate from the skirt. The jacket bodice was

173

close-fitting and buttoned down the front. There was also a garment known as a *gilet-cuirasse* which looked like a man's waistcoat and was sometimes a separate garment and sometimes joined to the jacket. Skirts were made to stand out by lining, and sometimes there was an additional woollen interlining added to the upper part of the skirt at the back. Many petticoats were worn, and what might be described as the tea-cosy effect was further emphasized by the use of a small bustle made of horsehair. This, to the confusion of modern students, was known as a 'crinoline'. It was quite different from the crinoline of the future, but etymologically the term was more correct than when it was applied to the steel hoops of the 1850s and 1860s, for *crin* is the French for 'horsehair', and that was the substance of which the early 'crinolines' was made. Skirts were nearly always adorned with flounces, which might be double or multiple, or else with ruching and other decoration.

Scholars distinguish four types of day dresses – the pelisse-robe, the redingote, the round dress and the peignoir – but there was a considerable amount of confusion and overlapping, and by the end of the decade the first two terms were used indiscriminately. In general it may be said that the pelisse-robe was worn indoors in the morning, the redingote was used for the 'promenade', and the rather more decorated round dress was worn in the afternoon. The peignoir was an informal dress worn only in the morning, but it was not in the modern sense of the word a dressing-gown.

Evening dresses were décolleté, off the shoulder and either straight across or with a slight dip in the middle. The term for the latter was *en cœur*. The horizontal pleats across the top of the corsage are very typical of this period, as was also the deep 'bertha' which fell from the top of the corsage to halfway down the sleeves and was made up of lace and frills or ribbon. The body of the bodice came to a point in front and was strongly boned. The favourite materials for day dresses were broadcloth, merino, foulard, organdie, gingham and tarlatan. Evening dresses were usually made of shot silk or velvet.

Outdoor garments were of various types. The shawl had now come back into favour and was sometimes very large with a fringed border. Paisley shawls were no longer considered a mere substitute for imported cashmere, for the Queen's residence at Balmoral had brought all things Scottish into favour. Various new forms of the cloak were invented, and were given different names according to whether they had capes, sleeves or slits through the arms or all three together. The differences between casawecks, polkas and pardessus were trifling; the names are a reminder of the influence at this time of some of the costumes of Eastern Europe, particularly those of Hungary.

Everything was done at this period to make women look as small as possible, partly perhaps in deference to Queen Victoria, who was of diminutive stature. Footwear, with rare exceptions, was therefore made without heels. The usual form was the slipper, sometimes laced over the ankles like that of a ballerina but without the reinforced toe. Such slippers were made of silk or crêpe in colours matching the dress. Very small feet were admired as a mark of gentility. In the street it was customary to wear cloth boots with elastic sides, but genteel ladies did not venture much abroad. By 1850, mid-Victorian modes, for men and women, seemed to have set in a mould. Those who wore them saw no reason why they should ever change.

Mantles for the
theatre, 1835

LE FOLLET

193 Day dresses, 1853. The skirt with many flounces is very typical of the early 1850s. Its shape is maintained by a multiplicity of petticoats, the crinoline not yet having been brought in to support it

CHAPTER EIGHT

From 1850 to 1900

AFTER the Hungry Forties, the bustling, prosperous Fifties. The Year of Revolutions (1848) had resulted in the defeat of the Left all over Europe. In some countries this had resulted in the re-establishment of centralized tyranny; but in England and France it was really the triumph of the *bourgeoisie*. It is true that the *coup d'état* of Louis Napoleon in 1851 gave rise to some anxiety, but in spite of his military adventures later in the decade, the real supporters of Napoleon III were the bankers, industrialists and capitalists. In England the Great Exhibition of 1851 not only demonstrated new kinds of technology but gave hope (a misguided hope as it turned out) that an era of universal peace and brotherhood was about to begin. Trade and commerce were certainly flourishing. We have only to look at the immense number of houses in London with stucco fronts and a portico with two pillars, nearly all of them built in the 1850s, to realize that the London businessman and merchant now had enough money to cease living 'over the shop' in the City and retire to the gentility of South Kensington and Belgravia.

Increasing prosperity meant an increasing elaboration of dress, and we find R. S. Surtees, in one of his novels (*Ask Mamma*, 1853), complaining that 'the housemaid now dresses better – finer at all events – than her mistress did twenty years ago, and it is almost impossible to recognize working people when they are in their Sunday dresses'. Skirts continued to expand, and for the first half of the decade the desired effect was obtained by wearing underneath them a larger number of petticoats. The weight of these finally became intolerable, and in 1856 they were replaced by a 'cage crinoline' or hooped petticoat.

194 *A Windy Corner*, 1864. The crinoline is now worn by every woman, and even by the little girl pushing the primitive perambulator

This was not, of course, the first time that skirts had been supported by hoops. We have already noted the clumsy cartwheel farthingale of the Elizabethan period and the side panniers of the eighteenth century, but the new crinoline was a much more scientific apparatus, for technology was now sufficiently advanced for the manufacturers to be able to supply *Ill. 196* flexible steel hoops which could either form a separate garment, hung by tapes from the waist, or be sewn into a petticoat.

When the crinoline was first invented, it must have seemed to women an instrument of liberation. No longer hampered by multiple layers of petticoat, they could, inside their steel cage, move their limbs freely. Of course there was a danger in this, and the caricaturists of the period delighted to show what could happen to crinolined ladies 'in a high wind'. Legs were still supposed to be invisible, and in case of mischance it was customary to wear long linen pantaloons edged with lace and sometimes reaching to the ankle. Little girls also wore *Ill. 195* these pantaloons in spite of the fact that their skirts were comparatively short. Indeed, it became a mark of gentility for the lace pantaloons to be seen. Mothers who could not afford the complete garment had to be content with what were called 'pantalettes', which were simply tubes of white linen ending just above the knee. These strange compromise garments were sold in enormous numbers.

It seems to be one of the principles of fashion that once an exaggeration has been decided on it becomes ever more exaggerated. Thus, by the end of the decade, the crinoline-supported skirts were truly prodigious, until it was impossible for two women to enter the room together or sit on the same sofa, for the frills of one dress took up all available space. A woman was now a majestic ship, sailing proudly ahead, while a small tender – her male escort – sailed along behind.

195 Girls in crinoline dresses and pantaloons, 1853

196 Crinoline petticoat, c. 1860. The crinoline is circular in form and consists of eight hoops of flexible steel wire

All this did not pass without protest. Even before the crinoline had come into being there were rumours from America of a new movement for a rational dress for women. The formidable
Ill. 199 Mrs Bloomer came to England in 1851 to spread her gospel and to try to induce women to adopt her sensible and certainly not unfeminine costume. This consisted of a simplified version of the bodice in vogue, and a fairly ample skirt which reached well below the knee. Underneath it, however, were to be seen baggy trousers reaching to the ankle, usually with a lace frill at the bottom. This very modest attempt to reform female dress provoked an almost unbelievable outburst of excitement,

197 Paris fashions for September 1859

198 *In a box at the Opera*, from *Le Follet*, 1857. The woman who is not décolleté is presumably a maid or theatre attendant

199 Mrs Amelia Bloomer, c. 1850. Mrs Bloomer's very modest attempts to reform female dress met with a storm of hostility and ridicule

200 Right, *Une tournure à faire tourner toutes les têtes!*, by Charles Vernier. The silhouette of male and female costume has never differed more drastically than in 1860

ridicule and vituperation. What might be called the trouser complex came into full play. Women were endeavouring, it seemed, to 'wear the trousers', and the mid-Victorian man regarded this as an outrageous attack on his own privileged position. *Punch*, that faithful mirror of middle-class opinion in the nineteenth century, brought out dozens of cartoons emphasizing the consequences of a possible sexual revolution, a world in which timid men were in complete subjection to their bloomered spouses.

As the husband, shall the wife be; he will have to wear a gown
If he does not quickly make her put her Bloomer short-coats down.

However, as an attempt to influence contemporary fashion, the Bloomer Movement was a complete failure. A few 'advanced' ladies adopted the costume, but the upper classes refused to have anything to do with it, and Mrs Bloomer had to wait for almost fifty years before she had her revenge in the adoption of 'bloomers' for cycling.

Her attempt was premature, for the mid-nineteenth century was the high-water mark of male domination, and in such patriarchal periods the clothes of the two sexes are as clearly differentiated as possible. A visitor from Mars contemplating a man in frock coat and top hat and a woman in a crinoline might well have supposed that they belonged to different species. And the crinoline certainly bore a symbolic relation to the age in which it thrived. In one of its aspects it symbolized female fertility, as an expansion of the apparent size of the hips always seems to do. This was an age of big families, and since the rate of infant mortality was not quite so high as it had been in previous periods, the population of England expanded rapidly.

In another sense the crinoline was a symbol of the supposed unapproachability of women. The expanded skirt seemed to say: 'You cannot come near enough to me even to kiss my hand.' But of course the enormously expanded skirt was a hollow sham; it was itself an instrument of seduction. As I have written elsewhere, 'when we see engravings of ladies with skirts like old-fashioned tea-cosies we are apt to think of the structure as solid and immovable; but, of course, nothing was further from the truth. The crinoline was in a constant state of *Ill. 200* agitation, thrown from side to side. It was like a rather restless captive balloon, and not at all, except in shape, like the igloo of the Eskimos. It swayed now to one side, now to the other, tipped up a little, swung forward and backward. Any pressure on one side of the steel hoops was communicated by their elasticity to the other side, and resulted in a certain upward shooting of the skirt. It was probably this upward shooting which gave mid-Victorian men their complex about ankles, and it certainly resulted in a new fashion in boots' (*Taste and Fashion*). Throughout the Forties the footwear of women had been reduced to a heelless slipper, scarcely seen among the voluminousness of the dress; but now boots came in, with higher heels and laced half-way up towards the calf. The crinoline was certainly not a moral garment, and the period in

184

201 *The Empress Eugénie and her maids of honour*, by F. X. Winterhalter, *c.* 1860

which it reached its greatest development, Second Empire France, was not a moral period. The social history of the Second Empire is the history of the *grande cocotte*.

There certainly seems to have been a symbolic relationship between the crinoline and the Second Empire, with its material prosperity, its extravagance, its expansionist tendencies – and its hypocrisy. And the Queen of the Crinoline was the Empress Eugénie herself. She was perhaps the last Royal personage to have a direct and immediate influence on fashion, and the crinoline suited her style to perfection. It was never more proudly or effectively displayed than during her reign. And now a new race of fashion designers had arisen to transform the whole world of *haute couture*.

Ill. 201

202 Crinoline dress by Worth, *c.* 1860. As Worth could not draw, he had lithographs made of heads and arms and then sketched in the dress

In former ages the fashion designer had been a comparatively humble person, visiting ladies in their homes. And the vast majority of them had been women. Now M. Worth, who, in spite of being an Englishman, had in ten years made himself a dictator of the mode in Paris, required ladies (with the exception of Eugénie and her Court) to come to *him*. The French historian Hippolyte Taine has described the scene, as ladies, anxious to be dressed by Worth, waited upon him in his salon.

'This little dry, black, nervous creature sees them in a velvet coat, carelessly stretched out on a divan, a cigar between his lips. He says to them, "Walk! turn! good! come back in a week, and I will compose you a toilette which will suit you." It is not they who choose it, it is he. They are only too happy to let him do it, and even for that need an introduction. Mme B., a personage of the *Beau Monde* and elegant to boot, went to him last month to order a dress. "Madame", he said, "By whom are you presented?" "I don't understand." "I'm afraid you must be presented in order to be dressed by me."

203 London and Paris fashions for June 1864. The crinoline has begun to slip to the back and is no longer a perfect circle

She went away, suffocated with rage. But others stayed, saying, "I don't care how rude he is so long as he dresses me." ' Worth soon had innumerable imitators, but few or none equalled his *panache* or his success.

The crinoline lasted for about fifteen years and in that time went through several modifications. It reached its greatest extent about the year 1860. At that time it projected as much to the front as to the back. The skirt looked like a bee-hive, not only from the front but from the side. Waists were tight, and the bodice was fitted to the figure; but out of doors it was the custom to wear a shawl or mantalette, with the result that a woman's general appearance was that of a broad-based triangle, the effect being enhanced by the smallness of the bonnet, which had now begun to slip back from the forehead to reveal the front hair. Then, in the mid 1860s, the crinoline began to slip *Ill. 203*   to the back of the skirt, leaving the front more or less straight, and in 1868 there was a further change, the reinforcement of the skirt having slipped entirely to the back and being indeed no more than a half-crinoline. There was a mass of material at the back, ending in a train, and when the crinoline was removed altogether, towards the end of the Sixties, this was looped up into a kind of bustle, the characteristic of the next decade. The crinoline, in fact, having served as a symbol of the Second Empire, collapsed with it like a pricked balloon. In the street it was the fashion for younger women to wear a shorter skirt, which could be looped up by means of strings to reveal a skirt underneath, but this was a very temporary fashion, the skirts of the Seventies being excessively long and trailing.

The defeat of France in 1870 and the troubles of the following year kept Paris out of the picture for a while, and it was some time before she recovered her ascendancy. Contemporary writers saw a return to a greater simplicity, though to our eyes the dresses of the early 1870s seem voluminous and luxurious enough. They even seem a little garish, an effect to which two recent inventions contributed. One was the sewing machine, and the other the introduction of aniline dyes. Gone were the

188

204 *Women in the garden*, by Claude Monet, 1866–7. Even in light
summer dresses the crinoline was still considered essential

subdued soft colours of the former decade, their place being taken by all kinds of bright hues. It was the fashion to have the bodice of a different colour from the skirt and to cut the dress out of two different materials, one patterned and one plain, the plain portion of the dress being trimmed with the patterned material and the patterned portion being trimmed with the plain. The effect was sometimes that of a patchwork quilt, and a writer in the magazine *The Young Englishwoman* (1876) complains that 'it is now impossible to describe dresses with exactitude: the skirts are draped so mysteriously, the arrangements of trimmings is usually one-sided and the fastenings are so curiously contrived that if I study any particular toilette for even a quarter of an hour the task of writing down how it is all made remains hopeless.'

LE JOURNAL DES MODES.

205 Left, London and Paris fashions for March 1869. The silhouette is now straight down the front and the crinoline is about to give place to the bustle

206 Headdresses, 1870

Bonnets had now given way to hats, very small hats perched   *Ill. 206* over the forehead and worn on top of a mass of hair which now formed an enormous chignon of plaits or curls. So much hair was required for this new fashion that many women were unable to provide it themselves, and enormous quantities of hair was imported and made up into 'scalpettes' and 'frizzettes'. Seen from the side, the shape of the back of the hair was a curious echo of the shape of the back of the skirt.

The dresses were of two kinds: those which were all in one piece (the so-called 'Princess' style) and those which consisted of a separate bodice and skirt. The jacket bodice was carried over from the previous decade and was made with short basques or with long basques forming a kind of overskirt. A loose skirt in a contrasting material or colour was sometimes worn with this garment; and a similar effect was obtained from the cuirasse bodice, which came in about 1874 and often had a plastron of different material down the front. The cuirasse bodice was very tight and moulded to the hips. This necessitated the use of a long, tight corset, and ladies who did not wish to encase themselves in this in the home wore a blouse. Sleeves were in general tight. An overskirt was sometimes used; it was draped at the sides in various ways, and in the early 1870s was, as we have seen, bunched out at the back into a bustle.

El David Dees Paris

Imp Lemercier &Cⁱᵉ de Seine St Paris

The Duke of Edinburgh.   The Grand Duchess Marie Alexandrovna.

207 Fashion plate from the *Tailor and Cutter, c.* 1870. A curious example of the practice at this period of sticking the heads of well-known people on a fashion plate

208 Lady's and child's dresses, September 1873, from the *Journal des Demoiselles*

The 'Princess' style was capable of considerable variety, one of the most popular of which was the polonaise, sometimes buttoned all down the front. The popularity of Dickens's *Barnaby Rudge* brought in the 'Dolly Varden' dress. It was usually of brightly patterned chintz or cretonne, and was fondly imagined by its wearers to be some kind of eighteenth-century costume. It was worn with a picture hat tilted forward over the forehead. At the end of the decade a knitted costume came in. It was made fashionable by Mrs Langtry, the 'Jersey Lily', and was therefore known as the 'jersey dress'. Another variety was the tea gown, which was loose enough to allow corsets to be discarded. Originally intended as a *robe de chambre* – and the name indicates its French origin – it had become very elaborate by the late 1870s, with many frills and flounces and much lace. *Ill. 208* It was essentially a matron's gown, and a lace cap was always worn with it.

209 *Madame Moitessier*, by J.-A.-D. Ingres, 1844/5–56

210 *Derby Day*, by
William Powell Frith,
1856–8

211 *Omnibus Life
in London*, by
William Egley,
1859. In the
mid-century the
crinoline was still
in full swing in
spite of the
inconvenience of
squeezing it into
the narrow
confines of an
omnibus

212 Ladies' and child's costume, March 1877

Ills. 212, 213

By the middle of the decade the bunched-up bustle had disappeared. The skirts were still full at the back, but the fullness was lower down, and even day dresses were provided with a surprisingly long train – to the disgust of Ruskin and others, who pointed out how very unhygienic such a style must necessarily be. Skirts were extremely hampering and, about 1876, we find in *Punch* a whole series of cartoons depicting ladies whose dress was so tight that they could neither sit down nor climb stairs. The waist was ferociously tight-laced, and it was made to look even smaller by wearing the corset, so to speak, outside, as part of the bodice running down to a sharp

213 Evening dresses, c. 1877

point in front. This became the prevailing mode in the early 1880s, the skirt emerging underneath the corset bodice being horizontally draped to make the waist look smaller still. In the mid 1880s there was a revival of the bustle, but it was of a different kind. It stuck out horizontally from the small of the back, but the supporting structure was no longer, as it had been in the early 1870s, a contrivance of horsehair. We find advertisements of 'the braided wire health bustle, warranted to be less heating to the spine than any others'. There was also the 'Langtry' bustle, an arrangement of metal bands working on a pivot. It could be raised when sitting down and sprang back automatically into place when the lady rose to her feet! One of the most extraordinary inventions in the whole history of fashion.

Ills. 214–15

Ill. 218

214 Left, *Too Early*, by
James Tissot, 1873. The
gentleman in the
doorway has brought
his 'gibus' (crush hat)
into the ballroom, as
was the custom

215 *La Grande Jatte*, by
Georges Seurat, 1884–6.
The bustle of the
mid 1880s is quite
different from the
bustle of the 1870s

216 Evening and
visiting dress, 1884. The
extreme form of the
second bustle built over
a horsehair or wire
frame

One cannot omit from a study of the fashions of the 1880s
Ill. 217 some reference to Aesthetic costume, although it was never
worn by more than a small section of the community. It was
intended as a protest against the ugliness of contemporary
fashion, but none the less followed its essential line. Aesthetic
dress was looser and had larger sleeves, and those who wore it
imagined that they were clothing themselves in some kind of
medieval or Renaissance costume. The comparatively loose
robe was embroidered with large sunflowers. The Aesthetic
lady wore no corset, had heelless shoes and brushed her hair
forward over her eyes. The Aesthetic dress was attractive
enough for those who had the figure for it, but the majority of
its wearers were not so favoured, and *Punch* once again made
merry with their slouching walk and drooping shoulders. The
male Aesthetes (although the satirists pretended that they could
not really be male) affected knee-breeches, a velvet jacket, a
flowing tie and a wideawake hat. This was the costume worn
by Oscar Wilde when he went on his lecture tour of America,
and it was the costume worn by Bunthorne in Gilbert and
Sullivan's *Patience*, which set out to ridicule the whole Aesthetic
Movement.

217 *Nincompoopiana – The Mutual Admiration Society*, by George du
Maurier, 1880. Satire on the costumes and attitudes of the Aesthetes

218 Bustle advertisements. The horsehair bustles of the 1870s and the 'scientific' bustles of the 1880s. The 'Health Bustle' is recommended as being 'less heating to the spine than any others'. The 'Langtry' bustle folded up to allow the wearer to sit down and sprang into place again when she got up

219 *The Reception*, by James Tissot, 1886. No nineteenth-century painter is more useful to the costume historian than Tissot. He observed the *toilettes* of the period with the greatest attention and painted them with meticulous accuracy

220 *The Picnic*, by James Tissot, 1875. Informal clothes, painted in the garden of Tissot's own house in St John's Wood

Ordinary male costume at this period showed little change from that of the preceding decade. The cut-away coat was worn only in the evening and was embellished with black silk facings. For daytime the frock coat had now established itself as the accepted town wear. Another possibility was the morning coat, cut away in a curve over the hips and buttoning rather high over the chest. Among the young, the short jacket was becoming increasingly popular, particularly at Oxford and Cambridge. Double-breasted 'reefer' jackets were also worn, especially for yachting. The influence of sport is very noticeable at this period. All kinds of new sports were now coming into favour, and it was impossible to practise them with any comfort in the formal dress of the day. For shooting, a man could wear a Norfolk jacket, with its characteristic belt and vertical pleats,

221 *Les Parapluies*, by Renoir, *c.* 1884. Renoir is a very useful portrayer of ordinary middle- and working-class costume at this period

and rather loose knee-breeches with gaiters. The hat worn with
this outfit was of soft felt and sometimes had a dent in the
crown like the later homburg. Cricket costume was the same
as today, except that it was still permissible to wear a coloured
shirt. Bright-coloured blazers were now coming into fashion.

Ill. 222   For the new sport of cycling, which was still in the 'penny-
farthing' stage, an extraordinary costume was devised: tight-
fitting knee-breeches, a very tight, military-looking jacket and
a little pillbox cap. The really smart wearer of this outfit
carried a bugle to warn pedestrians of his approach. This
peculiar get-up does not seem to have been adopted in France
and Germany, where cycling was almost equally popular.

222 Male and female cycling
costume, 1878–80

223 Male and female seaside
costume, 1886

204

THE MILITARY.   THE PRINCESS.   CHESTERFIELD.   THE LOUNGE.

224 British spring and summer costume, 1884

The most popular overcoat was the chesterfield, which began *Ill. 224* by being knee-length but gradually grew longer; it was made of such materials as miltons, worsteds and cheviots, in black, brown, blue or grey. It usually had silk facings and was edged with braid. The top frock was almost a replica of the frock coat underneath, except, of course, that it was cut more loosely and was generally made of heavier material. The inverness and the ulster were capes, or rather half-capes, attached to a coat. A short double-breasted overcoat, with a shoulder cape sometimes trimmed with fur, was called the 'Gladstone' overcoat; another variety with a half-circle cape was known as the 'Albert'. In the evening the tail coat was still essential at all formal functions, but the dinner jacket was increasingly worn at home or when dining at the club. When the ladies had retired, it was permitted to put on a smoking jacket. This was similar in form to the dinner jacket, but was almost invariably quilted, presumably for warmth, since the smoking rooms and billiard rooms of country houses were often unheated.

There is little difference between male costume in the 1880s and in the 1890s, except for the increasing use of informal *Ill. 225* attire. It was still considered rather 'caddish' to wear anything but a frock coat or a morning coat in town, when paying calls or when taking part in the Sunday church parade in Hyde Park. Lounge suits could be of blue serge or patterned tweeds. With them it was quite permissible to wear a fancy waistcoat, sometimes extremely brightly patterned, although the *Tailor and Cutter* issued a warning in 1890 that 'gentlemen with abdominal convexity will use discretion in the employment of hues and patterns calculated to draw attention to that unromantic formation'. Trousers in the early 1890s were of the peg-top variety, and dashing young men began to wear them with turn-ups. These, however, were still looked on with disfavour, and it created quite a sensation when, in 1893, Viscount Lewisham appeared in the House of Commons wearing them.

Ties and bows could be adjusted in several ways. Sometimes they were ready-made. The height of the collar increased steadily throughout the decade until it became a real 'choker'.

The bustle finally disappeared from female costume, together with the horizontal skirt draperies so characteristic of the 1880s. Dresses were smooth over the hips and made to fit more snugly by being cut on the cross. Skirts were long and bell-shaped and usually had a train even when worn in the street. Day dresses were high in the neck and finished with ruching or a large bow of tulle. A good deal of lace was worn, even day blouses being elaborately adorned. Some evening gowns were made entirely of lace, and much was worn also on petticoats, which now assumed a new importance. Since it was impossible to cross the street without holding up the long skirt with one hand, the gesture inevitably displayed the lace frilling of the petticoat, which seems to have had at this period an

225 *Count Robert de Montesquiou,* by Giovanni Boldini, 1897

extraordinary amount of erotic appeal. Sleeves, which at the beginning of the decade were peaked at the shoulders but otherwise fairly narrow, had grown to enormous proportions by 1894. Some sleeves were so large that cushions were necessary to keep them in place. They were even thought essential in stage costume and fancy dress – a requirement which, on the stage, made any attempt at historical accuracy in period plays an impossibility.

Ill. 229

By now, the bicycle had become immensely popular. This made it inevitable that some kind of bifurcated garment should be worn, since it was impossible to ride a bicycle in a trailing skirt. Divided skirts were one solution and so were baggy knickerbockers called 'bloomers'. They caused almost as much excitement as the original bloomer campaign of the 1850s. They were ridiculed in the Press and denounced in the pulpit, but it was all to no avail; young women continued to wear them. Indeed, the new enthusiasm for outdoor sports of all kinds made it necessary to wear more rational garments in general and there was a new vogue for the tailored suit, consisting of jacket, skirt and 'shirtwaister'. The odd thing is that

Ill. 226

226 Cycling dress, March 1894

227, 228 Left, in the garden, 1891. Right, riding costume, February 1894

when women went in for outdoor pursuits they insisted on wearing men's hats and men's stiff white collars. Sports clothes for women were in general heavy, made of homespuns or tweeds, and the colours were usually dark. *Ill. 228*

Hats throughout the decade were rather small and perched squarely on the top of the head. Outdoor garments consisted of mantles, cloaks and capes, the first two terms being more or less interchangeable. The cape, however, was usually shorter, fitted closely over the shoulders and reached to the waist. The early mantles often had medici collars up to the ears, kept in position by means of wires. Many women wore the masculine chesterfields and three-quarter-length coats. Shoes had comparatively high heels and rounded toes and were laced up the front. Boots could be laced or buttoned. They were made of leather or cloth. Stockings were nearly always black, of lisle

209

229 Autumn walking dress, 1895   230 At the races, 1894
Examples of the extreme form of the balloon sleeve in the mid 1890s

thread in the daytime and silk in the evening. In the evening
it was fashionable to wear very long suede gloves, sometimes
with as many as twenty buttons, and to carry a very large fan
of curved or straight ostrich feathers. Jewellery was extensively
Ill. 232   worn. Colours in general were rather bright and discordant,
the favourite of all being yellow. It is no accident that the
most exciting publication of the decade was called *The Yellow
Book.*

Political events were not without their effect on fashion.
The dominance of Paris was still unquestioned, and the French
Government was now inclined to ally itself with Russia. The
Russian fleet visited Toulon in 1893, and three years later the
Tsar himself came to Paris amid scenes of the greatest en-
thusiasm. This inaugurated a vogue for furs, which were

231 Travelling costume, 1898   232 Walking dress, February 1899

adopted by women as well as by men: in former ages fur had been almost entirely a male prerogative. The position was now somewhat reversed, in that women wore furs in the form not only of trimmings, but of whole fur coats, whereas men's fur coats had the fur on the inside, the fur being visible only in the collar and the cuffs.

The 1890s as a whole was a period of changing values. The old, rigid society-mould was visibly breaking up, with South African millionaires and other *nouveaux riches* storming the citadels of the aristocracy. For the young there was a new breath of freedom in the air, symbolized both by their sports costumes and by the extravagance of their ordinary dress. It was perfectly plain that the Victorian Age was drawing to its close.

233 *The Wertheimer Sisters*, by John Singer Sargent, *c.* 1901

From 1900 to 1939

THE PERIOD from the beginning of the century to the outbreak of World War I is usually spoken of in England as the Edwardian era, although the King actually died in 1910. In France, with a slight extension backwards into the middle of the 1890s, it was referred to as *la belle époque*. In both countries the atmosphere was very similar. It was an age of great ostentation and extravagance. In England, society and the Court, which had of course always overlapped, now began to coincide and the King himself set the example. As Virginia Cowles remarks, 'The fact that the King liked City men, millionaires, Jewish jokes and American heiresses and pretty women (regardless of their origin) meant that the doors were open to anyone who succeeded in titillating the Monarch's fancy. . . . Edwardian society modelled itself to suit the King's personal demands. Everything was larger than lifesize. There was an avalanche of balls and dinners and country house parties. More money was spent on clothes, more food was consumed, more horses were raced, more infidelities were committed, more birds were shot, more yachts were commissioned, more late hours were kept, than ever before' (*Edward VII and His Circle*, London 1956).

Fashion as always reflected the age. Like the King himself it favoured the mature woman, cool and commanding with a rather heavy bust, the effect of which was further emphasized by the so-called 'health' corsets which, in a laudable effort to prevent a downward pressure on the abdomen, made the body rigidly straight in front by throwing forward the bust and throwing back the hips. This produced the peculiar S-shaped stance so characteristic of the period. The skirt, smooth over the hips, flared out towards the ground in the shape of a bell.

234 Evening dress: *Il a été primé*. Fashion plate from *La Gazette du Bon Ton*, 1914

235 *Madame Jasmy Alvin*, by Kees van Dongen, 1928

Cascades of lace descended from the corsage; indeed there was a passion for lace in every part of the gown. For those who could not afford real lace there was a considerable vogue for Irish crochet. The hair was built high on the head, and the flat pancake hat projected forward as if to balance the train. In the evening the dresses were extravagantly décolleté, but in the daytime the whole body was concealed from the ears to the feet. The little lace collar was kept in place by boning, and the arms were always completely concealed by long gloves. There was a rage for feathers, hats being adorned with one or more plumes; feather boas were worn round the neck. The best examples were made entirely of ostrich plumes and sometimes cost as much as ten guineas.

236, 237 Left, spring dresses trimmed with silk braid and with lace, May 1900

238 Straight-fronted corset, February 1902

239 Chiffon dress, 1901

240 Evening dress, September 1901

THE
W.H.K&S
"ASCOT"
STRAIGHT FRONTED
CORSET

241 Summer dress, *c.* 1903

242 Silk evening dress, 1911

243 Evening dress with lace, 1907–8

Photographs of the actual dresses, showing the texture of the materials

218

244 So-called 'Merveilleuse' dresses produced a sensation at the Longchamps races in May 1908. It was a strange delusion that these dresses resembled in any way the flimsy 'Empire' costumes of the 1790s

245 Dress of 1908. The period of the 'Gibson Girl', with heavy bust and swirling skirt

One sometimes wonders if the climate of Europe was very much better in the early years of the century than it has been since: so many of the clothes of the period look as if they had been designed for a garden party or to be worn at a Riviera casino. In the winter the greater part of smart society seems to have swarmed over to Monte Carlo and similar Mediterranean resorts. Whatever the ups and downs of the *entente* in political circles, it was plain that the English upper classes, once more following the example of the King, regarded France and England as parts of the same civilization, stamping grounds for the same round of pleasure. The period has been defined as 'the last good time of the upper classes', and even the colours of clothes reflected the sunny optimism of those that had money to spend. It was all pastel shades of pink, pale blue or mauve, or black with small sequins sewn all over it. The favourite materials were crêpe de chine, chiffon, *mousseline de soie* and tulle. Many satin dresses were embroidered in floral patterns with little clusters of ribbon, or even painted by hand. The amount of sheer labour which went into the making of one fashionable gown was truly prodigious; one would have to go back to the embroidered brocades of the early eighteenth century to find anything comparable.

The blouse had now become an extremely elaborate confection. It was adorned with tucking and insertion. 'Some blouses', says a writer in a contemporary fashion magazine, 'have circular trimmings of fluted muslin, giving a pretty graceful curve, and the trimming has a very fussy look.' The bolero was extremely popular, as was also the so-called Eton bodice, a garment like a boy's Eton jacket. The balloon sleeves of the 1890s had now been completely abandoned, sleeves in general being tight at the wrist and rather long so as to extend half over the hand. The tea gown, once merely a means of 'getting into something loose', was now an artistic creation in its own right.

Another feature of this period, however, is the importance of tailor-mades. A considerable number of young women of

246 Lady's golfing costume, 1907   247 Day dress, 1907

the middle classes were now beginning to earn their living as governesses, typists and shop assistants, and it would have been impossible for them to pursue their occupations in the elaborate garden-party dresses we have been describing. Even rich women wore tailor-mades in the country or when travelling, and the English tailors, rightly reputed to be the best in the world, reaped a rich harvest.

Ills. 246–7

For men the accepted wear for all formal occasions was still the top hat and the frock coat, but the lounge suit worn with a homburg hat (a name derived from the German spa, much visited by the Prince of Wales) was increasingly to be seen, even in the West End of London. Straw hats were extremely popular and were sometimes worn even with riding breeches; trousers

221

tended to be rather short and very narrow, and young men were beginning to wear them with permanent turn-ups and with a sharp crease in front, which had become possible since the mid 1890s with the invention of the trouser-press. Collars of white starched linen were extremely high and sometimes went right round the throat. This was an echo, as it were, of the boned necks of female attire.

Ill. 244

The female silhouette began to be slightly modified in 1908. The bust was no longer thrust quite so far forward, nor the hips so far back. Floppy blouses hanging over the waist in front were abandoned. The fashionable 'Empire' gown, although bearing very little resemblance to the dresses worn in the time of Napoleon I, had the effect of narrowing the hips. This can be seen quite plainly in the corset advertisements of the period. Hats became wider, which had the effect of making the hips look narrower still.

248 Far left, male summer costume, July 1907

249 Left, walking dress, 1910

250 Right, lady's motoring costume, April 1905. In the open motor-cars of the period it was necessary to be protected from cold and, above all, from dust

251 Flannel suit for boating, July 1902

252 Male motoring costume, c. 1904

And then, in 1910, there was a fundamental change in female dress. There has been much argument as to what brought this about, but it was plain that the Russian Ballet had something *Ills. 257–9* to do with it, and so had Paul Poiret, and we need not trouble ourselves with the question of which came first. What is certain is that there was a wave of Orientalism following the extraordinary excitement caused by the production of *Schéhérazade*, the costumes for which were designed by Leon Bakst. The colours were striking, even garish, and society adopted them with enthusiasm. The old pale pinks and 'swooning mauves' were swept away; the rigid bodices and bell-shaped skirts were abandoned in favour of soft drapery. Skirts became narrow at the hem, and in 1910 extremely so, *Ill. 253* resulting in the hobble skirt which made it difficult for a woman to take a step of more than two or three inches. To prevent women from taking a longer stride and so splitting the skirt, a fetter made of braid was sometimes worn.

253, 254 Emancipated woman:
Hobble-skirt dresses and
hobble garter, 1910

255, 256 The new silhouette, still heavy above but tapering towards the feet, seen at race meetings in 1914

It was as if every woman – and this in the very year of the Suffragette demonstrations – was determined to look like a slave in an Oriental harem. Some women even went so far as to wear little 'harem' trousers visible below the hem of the skirt, but these created such a sensation when worn in the street that only the most daring persisted. We can note here the obvious influence of the Russian Ballet, and the creations of Paul Poiret. With the extremely narrow skirt went very large hats. The silhouette, in complete contrast to that of the woman of 1860, was a triangle standing on its point. The favourite trimming of dresses was no longer lace but buttons, which were sewn all over, even in the most unlikely places.

225

258–60 Three costumes by Poiret showing Oriental influence. Left, 'Robe Sorbet', 1911; centre and right, dresses of 1913

In 1913 came another startling change. Dresses no longer had collars coming up to the ears; instead there was what was known as the 'V-neck'. This created an extraordinary amount of excitement. It was denounced from the pulpit as something very like indecent exposure and by doctors as a danger to health. A blouse with a very modest triangular opening in the front was dubbed a 'pneumonia blouse', but in spite of all these protests the V-neck was soon generally accepted. The collar, if there was one, now took the form of a small medici collar at the back of the neck.

257 At home, 1913. The graceful mode of the period just before World War I

Pre-war fashions:

261 Day dress, 1912

262 Evening dress by
Paquin, 1913

263 Day dress, 1914

264, 265 Utility clothes, World War I

Just before the outbreak of war there was another modification in the general outline of women's dress. Over the skirt,
which was very long and tight at the ankle, was worn another
skirt, a kind of tunic reaching to just below the knee. The
shape of hats also was modified. They were no longer excessively broad, but were small and fitted the head quite closely.
Feathers, which were still fashionable, were no longer curled
round the brim but stuck straight up into the air, and it was
customary to wear two feathers projecting at an angle. These
hats continued into the war period, but many women found
the double skirt an encumbrance in the war work in which
many of them were engaged. They therefore abandoned the
underskirt and wore the tunic or overskirt by itself. The   *Ill. 265*
simple tailor-made was also popular, many women feeling,
quite rightly, that extravagant dressing was out of place in
wartime. The war, in fact, as all wars do, had a deadening effect

on fashion, and there is little of interest to record until the conflict was over. For those who lived through the clothing restrictions and coupons of World War II, it is interesting to note that, in 1918, there was an attempt to introduce a National Standard Dress, a utility garment, with metal buckles instead of hooks and eyes, and designed, to quote a contemporary, as an 'outdoor gown, house gown, rest gown, tea gown, dinner gown, evening dress and nightgown'. Nightgown is surely the only surprising item in this list.

In 1919, when fashion picked up again, the flared skirt which had lasted throughout the war was replaced by the so-called 'barrel' line. The effect was completely tubular. Skirts were still long, but an attempt was made to confine the body in a cylinder. The bust was entirely boyish, and women even began to wear 'flatteners' in order to conform to the prevailing mode. The waist disappeared altogether, and there were already many examples of the waistline round the hips which was to be so characteristic a feature of the middle of the decade.

267 Right, evening dresses, 1919

266 Day dresses, June 1919

268 Left, day dresses and
velvet dress, 1921

269 Above, foulard silk
summer dress, 1920

The early 1920s: the line is
tubular but the skirt is still
long

231

And then, in 1925, to the scandal of many, came the real revolution of short skirts. They were denounced from the pulpit in Europe and America, and the Archbishop of Naples even went so far as to announce that the recent earthquake at Amalfi was due to the anger of God against a skirt which reached no further than the knee. The secular establishment was equally disturbed, especially in America, and, undeterred by the fact that sumptuary laws have had only minimal success throughout history, the legislators of various American States tried once more to impose their own view of morality. In Utah a Bill was brought in, providing fine and imprisonment for those who wore on the streets 'skirts higher than three inches above the ankle'; and a Bill introduced into the Ohio legislature sought to prohibit any 'female over fourteen years of age' from wearing 'a skirt which does not reach that part of the foot known as the instep'. It was all to no avail.

270 Summer dresses, 1926. The short skirt and the androgyne silhouette is now established

271 Ladies at
the Ritz,
April 1926

A new type of woman had come into existence. The new erotic ideal was androgyne: girls strove to look as much like boys as possible. All curves – that female attribute so long admired – were completely abandoned. And, as if to give the crowning touch to their attempted boyishness, all young women cut off their hair. The bob of the early 1920s was abandoned for the shingle, which made the coiffure follow much more closely the lines of the head. Even older women were compelled to conform, because the cloche hat, which had now become universal, made it almost impossible to have long hair. Early in 1927 even this was not considered enough, and the shingle was succeeded by the Eton crop. There was now nothing to distinguish a young woman from a schoolboy except perhaps her rouged lips and pencilled eyebrows.

A curious result of the new modes was that they notably diminished, or at least threatened, the dominance of the great Paris fashion houses. The Frenchwoman does not naturally look like a boy; she did not fit into the new fashions as easily as her contemporaries in England and the United States. As a commentator of the time remarked, 'the angular English woman, over whose lack of *embonpoint* papers like *La Vie Parisienne* have been making merry for two generations, now became the accepted type of beauty'. Several famous Paris firms, such as Doucet, Douillet and Drescoll, who had created the glories of *la belle époque*, closed their doors; and even Poiret, who had done so much to revolutionize fashion in 1910, now found himself completely out of tune with the times. New names emerged, many of them women. Madame Paquin, although she was head of a long-established firm, managed to conform to the new trend. Madeleine Vionnet accepted it with

L.2155.

enthusiasm; but the outstanding revolutionary talent of the
Twenties was undoubtedly 'Coco' Chanel, only rivalled a few *Ill. 274*
years later by the astonishing figure of Elsa Schiaparelli. These
two women were not merely dress designers; they formed an
important part of the whole artistic movement of the time.
Madame Chanel was an intimate friend of Cocteau, Picasso
and Stravinsky. Madame Schiaparelli was fantastically success-
ful, and it has been estimated that by 1930 the turnover of her
establishment in the rue Cambon was something like a hundred
and twenty million francs a year. Her twenty-six workrooms
employed more than two thousand people.

What the fashion people found so shocking about her was
her introduction of 'good working-class clothes' into polite
society. She was accused of having brought the *apache* into the
Ritz; but however simple her clothes might be, they always
had an elegance which made everyone admire and copy them.

272 Left, lady's tweed
suit, 1929

273 The 'flattener',
intended to abolish the
bust, 1924

274 Dresses by
Chanel, April 1926

275 At Chester races, 1926. Masculine elements in female costume

277 At the races, Longchamps, 1930.
The skirts are on the eve of going long
again and the waist is about to resume its
normal place

276 Afternoon coat, 1928

The function of fashion is to change, and by the end of the 1920s it was plain that a new style was about to be evolved. Skirts reached the extreme of shortness (the extreme, that is, until modern times) in 1927. It was not in everybody's interest that skirts should be short. It is true that the manufacturers of silk stockings were enjoying a boom, but the skimpy dresses of the period did not bring much profit to cloth manufacturers or the designers of accessories. It was plain that attempts were being made to bring skirts down again and, as so often happens, the first experiments were made with evening dress. Skirts remained short, but they were sometimes provided with a gauze overskirt which was somewhat longer; or long panels were added at the side. Another expedient, and an extremely ugly one, was to make the skirt longer at the back than the front. There were even examples which came down to the knees at the front and trailed on the ground behind, and this ugly and preposterous fashion lasted for nearly a year.

278 'Pierrette' hair-style
by Lanvin, 1928

279 Evening dress, May 1929. At the end of the 1920s the couturiers made definite efforts to bring in long skirts again by various devices such as transparent hems, side-pieces and trains

Then, as the decade drew to its close, skirts suddenly became long again and the waist resumed its normal place. It was as if fashion were trying to say: 'The party is over; the Bright Young Things are dead.' As in 1820, the return of the waist to its normal position symbolized a movement towards a new paternalism: in economic terms the American Slump; in political terms the rise of Hitler. The cloche hat, which had tyrannized over the mode for nearly ten years, was abolished and women were free to grow their hair again. The long sleeves were seen once more; but there is no exact parallel between the fashions of the early 1930s and those of a century before, for the waist did not become excessively tight and the general lines of the skirt remained more or less perpendicular. Wide

280, 281 Day and
evening dress by Lanvin,
1931

shoulders and slender hips seemed to be every woman's ideal, and this was exemplified in the figure of Greta Garbo, who in almost any earlier epoch would not have been considered a beautiful woman.

If the psychologists' theory of the Shifting Erogenous Zone can be accepted, once a focus of interest loses its appeal another one has to be found. In the early 1930s the emphasis shifted from the legs to the back. Backs were bared to the waist and, indeed, many of the dresses of the period look as if they had been designed to be seen from the rear. Even day dresses had a slit up the back, and the skirt was drawn tightly over the hips so as to reveal, perhaps for the first time in history, the shape of the buttocks.

282 Evening dress by Worth, 1930. An example of the new focus of erotic interest: a dress designed to be seen from the back

It seems likely that this backlessness had something to do with the evolution of bathing costumes. The bathing costumes of the 1920s were surprisingly modest; fashion photographs of the period show mannequins in quite ample overskirts and extremely limited décolletage. In the early 1930s all this was changed. What really brought this about, however, was not bathing, but *sunbathing*, which was now enjoying a tremendous vogue. If, as some fanatics claimed, the exposure of the skin to sunlight was the way to health for everybody, then obviously the greater portion of skin exposed the better. The overskirt of the bathing costume was therefore reduced to almost nothing, the armholes were enlarged and the décolletage was much deeper. Finally, the first backless bathing costume appeared, although, in fact, it was no more backless than the evening dress of the same period.

In addition to bathing, other sports were beginning to have a marked influence on ordinary costume, although we should note also the opposite tendency of sports clothes to develop a type of their own; this is particularly noticeable in the case of tennis. Most tennis players had simply worn the summer clothes of the period, even if the skirts were long and hampering to the movements. In the 1920s, when the skirts of ordinary dress were short, tennis costume followed suit, but when skirts became long again at the end of the decade, tennis dress went on, so to speak, on its own, since it was plainly absurd to reintroduce long skirts in what had now become a strenuous game. In April 1931 Señorita de Alvarez played in divided skirts which came to slightly below the knee, and two years later Alice Marble of San Francisco appeared in shorts above the knee. It was left to Mrs Fearnley-Whittingstall to appear at Wimbledon without stockings. This caused an uproar, but the new mode was so obviously sensible that it was soon adopted by almost all women players.

A similar evolution can be seen in skating costume, which by the early 1930s had crystallized into a kind of uniform, having a skirt with wide flares, at first knee-length but afterwards

283 Evening dress, 1932. Fashion drawing by Jean Maillart. More back-interest, and the enormous shoulder decoration foreshadows the square shoulders of the decade

much shorter. Cycling, although it had long ceased to have any appeal to the upper classes, was still extremely popular, and most young women adopted shorts, sometimes so short that considerable opposition was aroused when English cycling clubs went abroad.

The main lines of women's clothes in the early 1930s may be briefly summarized. Dresses were slim and straight, being sometimes wider at the shoulders than at the hips. Tall girls were admired, and all the tricks of the couturier were employed to give the impression of increased height. This effect can be *Ill. 283* increased by making the head look small, and so the hair was dressed rather close, with a small curl at the back of the neck.

243

284 At the races, 1930

285 Suit, 1935. An
extreme example of
the exaggerated
shoulder

286, 287 The bosom has not yet reasserted itself after the flat styles of the 1920s. Left, at the races, May 1935. Right, summer dress, 1934

On top was a gay little hat perched over one eye. Day dresses usually came to about ten inches above the ground, while evening dresses reached to the toes. Both evening and afternoon dresses were often provided with little capes. The bolero was extremely fashionable. Perhaps as a gesture of economy, evening dresses were sometimes made of woollen or cotton materials and even of broadcloth, previously thought suitable only for day wear.

Ill. 285

The Depression certainly helped to bring the clothes of the different classes closer together, at least in general line, and now a new process had begun which brought the creations of the great Paris houses within the reach of nearly every woman.

245

288, 289 'Butterfly' sleeve dresses, 1934

Before 1930 it had been the habit of buyers (especially American buyers) to purchase several dozen copies of each selected model shown in Paris and resell them to a wealthy clientele. But after the Slump the American authorities imposed a duty of up to 90 per cent on the cost of the original model. *Toiles* (i.e. patterns cut out in linen) were allowed in duty-free. Each *toile* was supplied with full directions for making it up, and although the original dress may have cost a hundred thousand francs, it was now possible to sell a simplified version for as little as fifty dollars. Another factor which contributed to the same end was the growing use of synthetic fabrics. Even the factory girl could now afford to purchase artificial silk stockings.

As the clouds of World War II began to gather, it became obvious that the fashionable silhouette was beginning to be modified, even if the fashion designers were as puzzled as the

290 Fashion shows in a salon, 1935

general public about what the dominating trend would be. There was a new wave of romanticism stimulated by the visit of the King and Queen to Paris in the early summer of 1938. 'Never', says C. Willett Cunnington, 'has Fashion been more ironic than in this attempt to revive, for an evening dress, the modes current on the eve of the Franco-Prussian War' (*English Women's Clothing in the Present Century*). There was even an attempt to revive the crinoline. Day dresses, however, showed an opposite tendency. The skirt was shorter and was bunched up in the peasant style. Curiously enough it was an *Austrian* peasant style, as if in unconscious acknowledgment of the growing power of Hitler. But right up to the eve of the conflict the majority of fashion designers, consciously or unconsciously, were betting that there would be no war. There was even an attempt to bring in tight-lacing again.

In the summer of 1939 *Vogue*'s reporter noted the extraordinary variety of models offered by the leading houses, and added: 'Nothing varies more than silhouette. You can look as different from your neighbour as the moon from the sun – and both of you are right. The only thing that you must have in common is a tiny waist, held in if necessary by super-lightweight boned and laced corsets. There isn't a silhouette in Paris that doesn't cave in at the waist.'

The accentuated waist was a boon to advertisers, who called upon women to 'control it with corsets . . . where there's a will there's a way!' Women were promised 'an old-fashioned boned, laced corset, made, by modern magic, light and persuasive as a whisper'. Perhaps, if peace had been preserved, women in the 1940s would once more have confined their waists in a rigid cage. History, however, decreed otherwise.

But for the moment it seemed that nothing had changed. Most of the great Paris houses launched their usual collections in the spring of 1940. It was the period of the 'phoney war', and no one in England or France or even America seemed to realize that the second great conflict of the twentieth century was really upon them.

248

292 Paris fashions, June 1939

291 At the races, 1938. Hats during the 1930s were a little mad in reaction against the universal cloche of the previous decade

293 Male fashions for
spring and summer, 1920

Men's clothes continued the progress towards informality which had been noticeable since the end of World War I. After the Armistice the frock coat had become something of a rarity, and its rival the morning coat was to be seen only at weddings, funerals or some occasion when Royalty was present. The lounge suit had now become ordinary town wear, but after 1922 it was shorter and had no slit up the back. The decay of the waistcoat led to a new increase in the popularity of double-breasted coats. The single-breasted coat, however, still continued, and in the later Twenties there was a craze for double-breasted waistcoats to go with it.

The chief change in the mid 1920s was in the width of trousers, the so-called 'Oxford bags'. It is thought that these may have originated from the extremely ample trousers made of towelling worn by undergraduate oarsmen *over* their shorts. It was customary for the coach to ride a horse along the tow-path wearing these trousers, and since he was a person of considerable prestige, undergraduates in general adopted the mode. Certainly they were to be seen everywhere, and were sometimes so wide that only the tip of the shoe was visible and the trousers flapped about the leg in the most extraordinary fashion. So strange a mode was not likely to last long, and by the end of the 1920s extremely wide 'Oxford bags' had disappeared, but trousers remained fairly wide until the end of the 1930s.

Meanwhile knickerbockers had been enjoying a renewed boom. For some obscure reason the breeches worn by Guards officers during World War I differed from the riding breeches of officers in Line Regiments by being extremely baggy and so loose as to hang over the top of the puttees. These had a strange effect on ordinary knickerbockers, which began to be cut, immediately after the war, in the same fashion, only even more amply. The new baggy knickerbockers were known as 'plus-fours', being considered especially suitable for golf. They completely drove out the old knickerbocker costume, which henceforward was worn only by old-fashioned intellectuals. They were in many ways the most typical sartorial invention of the period between the wars.

294 Examples of the new informality: left, M. Herriot in the French style; right, Mr Ramsay Macdonald in the English style, 1924

CHAPTER TEN

The last thirty years

THE FALL of France cut England off from the Continent
almost as completely as during the Napoleonic Wars. In Paris,
although the export trade was dead, the fashion houses continued to function and the Germans made every effort to
encourage the great couturiers to collaborate. Some of them
did so and produced clothes marked by an extreme exaggeration. After the war it was claimed that these had been a
deliberate attempt to make German women customers look
ridiculous, but this is to read back into history motives which
are unlikely to have been present at the time.

In England, clothes-rationing was introduced in June 1941,
and fashion almost ceased to exist. Women of all classes were
compelled to wear what clothes they already possessed, with
the occasional purchase of a few accessories. Any costume
distinction between the classes disappeared. Stockings were in
short supply, and many women began to go about with bare
legs; some of them even began to paint their legs and to draw
a line down the back to simulate the seam of the stocking. Many
young women took to wearing slacks, thus making stockings
unnecessary. Hats were replaced by headscarves and in wet
weather by plastic hoods. A curious exception to the general
look of austerity was the elaboration of hair-styles. It would have
been natural enough for girls working in factories to cut their
hair short, as had been done in the 1920s. On the contrary,
their bleached curls hung down to the shoulders, and this last
relic of luxury was passionately defended. One factory manager,
disturbed by the fact that nearly all his girl workers took one
day off during the week, called in an industrial psychologist.
This wise man suggested that a hairdressing salon should be

opened in the factory itself – and absenteeism miraculously ceased.

These austerity conditions affected all Europe. The British Board of Trade did what it could to keep up women's morale by encouraging the Fashion Group of Great Britain, which had been founded in 1925, to form an Incorporated Society; and this came about in 1942. The original members were Norman Hartnell, Peter Russell, Worth, Madame Mosca, Digby Morton, Victor Stiebel and Hardy Amies. They were later joined by Molyneux, Charles Creed and others. These designers, given the restrictions under which they worked, managed to produce some quite attractive 'Utility' garments. With these, women had to make do until the end of the war and for several years beyond.

295 Standard wartime gear with little hat, square shoulders and short skirt, and sensible shoes which often had wedge heels

When the war was over, French fashion made a determined attempt to reassert itself. With the encouragement of the Government, an exhibition called 'Le Théâtre de la Mode' was organized in 1945 at the Musée des Arts Décoratifs, and all the leading Parisian fashion designers took part, the list including such well-known names as Balenciaga, Balmain, Dior, Givenchy and Jacques Fath. Their designs for cocktail dresses with short, wide skirts, décolleté bodices, covered for the first part of the evening with a bolero, and even their designs for evening dresses, in the proper sense of the term, had considerable success in France and even more in the United States.

296, 297 Dresses by Lanvin, 1947. Anticipation of the New Look

298 Dior's New Look: suit
by Christian Dior, 1948

English women benefited very little by these developments;
it was not until early in 1949 that a large range of garments
became 'coupon-free', and there was still an acute shortage of
material. It was all the more astonishing, therefore, that in the
spring of 1947 they adopted Christian Dior's 'New Look'. This
was a deliberate attempt to break away from the short-skirted
tubular appearance with its square-padded shoulders which
had lasted since before the war. The new silhouette had narrow
shoulders, the waist in the right place, a new emphasis on the
bust and a longish skirt with a wide hem. This was a startling
innovation in more ways than one. Not only was it a complete reversal of fashion trends, but it provided the occasion

Ill. 298

for something that had never happened before in costume history: an attempt by the authorities to prevent women from wearing *more* clothes. In the past Church and State had often attempted to prevent women from wearing scanty garments on the ground that they were indecent. But the New Puritanism was concerned less with morality than with economics. Government disapproval, however, had no effect, and soon, all over Europe, women were wearing the 'New Look' or its equivalent.

It was, however, essentially a throw-back. It represented a desire on the part of women to return, after the austerities of wartime, to a more settled and, it was thought, more agreeable age. There was a curious parallel in the development of male garments: the so-called 'Edwardian' and 'Teddy Boy' clothes. It is important to distinguish between them.

The Edwardian modes were created by the bespoke West End tailors and were, as always, the reflection of the subconscious desires of those who wore them. At the corner of (say) Bond Street, it was possible to see a group of young men who seemed to have stepped bodily out of another epoch. They wore tight jackets buttoned high at the throat and rather long in the skirts, tight trousers and bowler hats with curly brims which looked as if they were just a size too small. An Edwardian of 1905 would not have noticed much difference between their clothes and his own. Never before in the long history of male costume had there been so obvious an attempt to wear the clothes of an earlier generation. Even the aristocrats who returned to Paris after the fall of Napoleon never attempted this deliberate abolition of an epoch. Neo-Edwardian clothes were a protest against Modernity, against the whole conception of the Welfare State and modern scales of taxation.

At the other end of the social scale were the 'Teddy Boys'. They were much attracted by the neo-Edwardian clothes, but they wore them with a difference; and each difference was designed to exaggerate their characteristics as men, to suggest, especially in their increased width of shoulder, that they were 'tough guys'. This was most apparent in the criminal fringes of society, in a world, in short, where individual prowess (real or supposed) is more important than membership of a class.

However, both the 'New Look' for women and the old look for men were in the nature of back-eddies, ripples on a stream which soon revealed its general direction. It has long been known to students of costume history that men's clothes almost always begin by being sports clothes. An obvious example is the dress of the Regency dandies, which plainly derived from the hunting costume of the late eighteenth century. The cut-away coat was originally designed for ease in sitting a horse; the top hat was a primitive crash-helmet. But, if men's clothes begin by being sports clothes, once they are adopted for ordinary wear, they begin to formalize themselves, to become smarter and better fitting – that is, tighter and less comfortable. By the 1840s what had originally been designed as a hunting costume had become 'evening dress', impossible for any active pursuit. It was therefore necessary to invent the 'lounge suit', and this in turn was formalized into what we now think of as correct 'city' wear. It would seem that at regular intervals, and especially after some great social upheaval, it is necessary to bring a new sports costume into everyday use.

This, once again, was what happened after World War II. The majority of young men, unless they were bank clerks or civil servants, began to wear sports clothes for the greater part of the day, and this development was much aided in the first years of peace by shops selling 'Government surplus stores'. This was something quite new. The uniforms of eighteenth- or nineteenth-century wars would have been quite unsuitable for civilian wear. Even after World War I it was merely a matter of an occasional trench coat or 'British warm': a knee-length overcoat which most officers preferred to the long greatcoat of the official issue. French and German uniforms seem to have had no influence on civilian dress.

But World War II was not fought in uniform proper, that is, not anything that George IV would have recognized as

257

uniform. It was fought in sports clothes; the battle-dress blouses were lumber jackets, and the only useful cap (the head-gear of the German Afrika Korps) was a skiing cap. Flying kit was an adaptation of the garments worn by Arctic explorers: it was never a uniform at all. And so, for the first time, clothing no longer used in war could be used in peace, especially for sport, without even the need to cut off fancy buttons.

The duffle-coat, invented by the Navy was worn after the war by all classes. Sometimes the coat was dyed, its natural beige transformed into dark blue, but the crude, if efficient, fastenings remained. Women, too, wore it – sometimes in blue, sometimes in other colours – and it was even taken up by the Paris fashion houses, who made it fit more closely to the figure.

The Army's battle-dress blouse, in various forms, was now a commonplace on the golf course, worn with corduroy trousers, plus-fours (that strange relic of World War I) having almost entirely disappeared. The Air Force provided the sleeve-

299 Military-style travelling-coat by Pierre Balmain, 1949

300 Sweater and skirt by Falaise, August 1954

301, 302 The
New Look in
evening and day
dresses: evening
dress by Mattli,
c. 1948, day dress
by Victor Stiebel,
1953

less leather coat and the kapok-stuffed jacket, both useful garments for the motor-cyclist. Sweaters of all kinds were
increasingly worn. Both men and women almost entirely
abandoned hats, except, paradoxically enough, for playing
games. The peaked cap generally adopted bore a marked
resemblance to that worn by the German Afrika Korps.

We have noted that the 'New Look' was a gesture of nostalgia
for a more settled time, a time when the middle classes had
servants and the life of a 'lady' was one of comparative idleness.
But it did not last, because women did not *really* want to go
back, that is, they were unwilling to sacrifice their new emancipation. Of this emancipation short skirts were the obvious
symbol. They meant that women had shaken off their shackles
and were 'stepping out'. They also meant a premium on youth;
it is no accident that all post-crisis clothes are 'little girls'
clothes'. Now if World War I meant a degree of female

303 Suit by Dior, 1957

emancipation, World War II meant that the emancipation was almost complete. 'New Look' clothes were obviously not the clothes of the emancipated woman as she had expressed herself in the 1920s. Writing in 1946 (*A Letter to a Girl on the Future of Clothes*), I ventured to suggest that by the end of the 1950s – that is, about ten years after the end of World War II (the amount of time needed for a post-crisis dress to emerge) – women would be wearing clothes similar to those they were wearing in the 1920s: straight in line, short in skirt, pale in colour and with the waist in the wrong place. And almost exactly ten years after his 'New Look' Dior launched his H-line, a short-skirted tubular dress with a low waist.

305 Trapeze dress by Dior, 1958. The transition from the New Look to the A-Line, with new emphasis on youth

304 Almost back in the 1920s: day dress by Jacques Griffe, 1958

306 Mary
Quant's first
'best seller',
1961

For a time women showed a certain reluctance to accept this, and two reasons can be adduced. One was the emphasis on the bosom which had been so evident in female fashion since the war, and the other is the curious psychological fact that it is impossible to admire any fashion again until it is thirty years old, that is, until a whole generation has elapsed. But when thirty years *had* elapsed (in this case, by the late 1950s), it was possible to revert frankly to the styles of the 1920s.

Skirts were short again, and by the mid-1960s they were very short indeed, shorter than they had been even in 1927, when they were just above the knee. Then, as we have noted, there was a reaction and by 1930 skirts were long again. Some commentators prophesied a similar reaction in modern times,

307 Right, outdoing the 1920s: the beginning of the mini-skirt, 1965

but in the Thirties there was a reason for it, a reaction in politics and economics, mirrored, as it always is, in the fashions of the time. This time the situation was different. There have been many waves of female emancipation in the past, but so far they have always retreated when their force was spent. It seems likely that what we are witnessing today is an *irreversible* wave of female emancipation, and if this is so, we may expect it to

308 Fashion envisages every kind of eccentricity: space-age clothes for the film *Maroc 7* by Clive, 1967

have a profound effect upon the clothes women wear. In periods of marked male domination the clothes of the two sexes are as different as possible. A hundred years ago, for example, women wore ample skirts supported by wide crinolines, and so long that only their toes were visible. Men wore top hats and frock coats and, of course, trousers. The two silhouettes were so dissimilar that the distinction between men and women was visible half a mile off. Today, an observer, walking a couple of yards behind a young man and a young woman, might well find it difficult to decide which was which. The hair is the same length, the upper part of the body is clothed

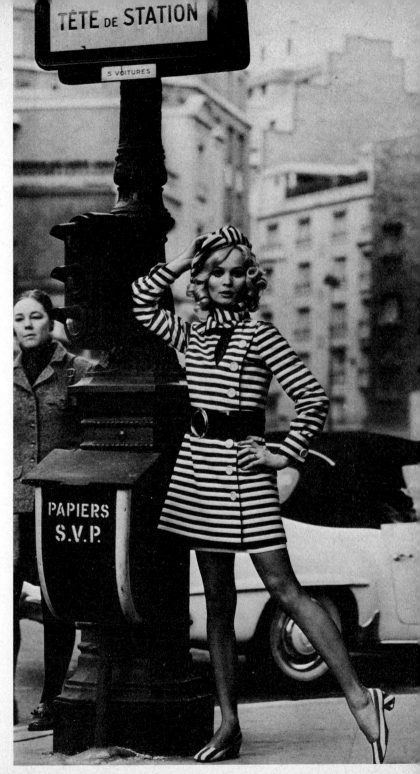

309 The
mini-skirt *in
excelsis*, 1968

in similar fashion and if the young woman is wearing trousers, the resemblance is complete.

Even if she is *not* wearing trousers but a mini-skirt, the outline is not very different. It almost seems as if women are abandoning the old idea of skirt and stockings and approaching something which might almost be called doublet-and-hose. Indeed a young woman of today bears the closest possible resemblance to a young man at the close of the medieval period, and an increasing number of young men, who no longer think it necessary to wear the traditional jacket, waistcoat and trousers, attain very much the same silhouette, i.e. the doublet-and-hose of (say) 1490. This means that they no longer care about formality and are no longer concerned to 'dress like a gentleman'. In other words, the idea of gentility which has kept men's clothes almost static for the last 150 years, is no longer accepted; and this represents a real revolution in manners. For nearly the whole of that period, all classes, except the very lowest, aspired to a 'gentlemanly' appearance. Even when men adopted sports clothes, the sports in question were the sports of the upper classes. This is no longer true. Many male garments of today seem to be derived from such 'lower-class' pastimes as riding a motor-cycle, or are altogether classless.

What this means is that, in Western society, the whole idea of gentility has broken down. It is true that those who work in banks, insurance offices and the like would certainly be in danger of losing their jobs if they came to work in unconventional garments; but this is not true of a whole wide range of modern occupations. Production managers and camera men in film and television studios are not in the least concerned to obey the old rules; pop singers even less so, and since these are the men who are most admired in the modern world, the influence of their example becomes more widespread every day.

It might be supposed that the decay of the idea of gentility would have an adverse effect on the London West End tailors, whose world-wide reputation, acquired in the time of Beau Brummell, was due to the excellence of their cutting and the

310 Men are beginning to resume their ruffles and long hair: Patrick Lichfield, 1968

fine materials of which their clothes were made. To a certain extent this has happened. In many of the clothes worn by young men today cutting is of less importance; they are not intended to sit closely to the figure; and the materials of which they are made include a large number of synthetic fabrics. As a result, bespoke tailors have been faced with a serious threat from an entirely new kind of men's outfitter. Savile Row has been challenged by Carnaby Street.

A few years ago, new names began to rival the prestige of the West End houses: Rupert Lycett Green, whose shop 'Blades' had such a success in London that he was able to open

a shop in New York as well; the photographer Patrick Lichfield; Michael Rainey, who designs all the clothes for his
engagingly named boutique 'Hung On You' (no one before
had ever heard of a *male* boutique). Young men like Ted
Dawson modelled their own clothes, the old prejudice against
male mannequins having faded away. The other prejudice that
the new clothes were worn only by homosexuals was also
disappearing, for some of their wearers were of a distinctly
masculine type; they were indubitably 'men'. Some of them
were even 'gentlemen', at least by descent and social background; but the point is that their clothes were not 'gentlemen's
clothes' in the old sense.

They were essentially classless clothes, which did not in the
least mean that they were cheap. They found plenty of buyers,
for young men of all classes now have money to burn, and they
spend a good deal of it on their own adornment. The designers
themselves set the example. In an interview one of them
admitted that he spent a fortune on his clothes: he had twenty-
six suits, a whole drawer full of sweaters (expensive to maintain
because they could be worn only two or three times before
being cleaned) and fifty shirts, some of them costing as much
as £6 apiece. He remarked, 'I don't understand people who
dress simply to keep warm . . . a man should enjoy his clothes.
A man doesn't dress for himself. He dresses to attract the girls.
. . . I have an idea that all men dress to be sexy, like cock
pheasants in the mating season.' This is a frank confession that
the Erotic Principle has returned to male dress after its long
eclipse.

It goes without saying that the Erotic Principle has, for almost
the whole of human history, been the dominant factor in
female dress. Men have chosen their partners in life for their
attractiveness as women, and therefore women's clothes are
designed to make women as attractive as possible. It would be
out of place in a short history of costume such as this to probe
too deeply into the psychological reasons for the clothes we
wear. None the less, some consideration is necessary.

Those who concern themselves merely with recording fashion's changes find themselves lost in an impenetrable jungle of facts. It is necessary to drive a road through the jungle, and this can be done only by trying to relate costume changes to historical and social events. It is now generally accepted that once 'fashion' had begun (which, as we have seen, took place some time in the fourteenth century), it could be made to yield its secret by discovering certain underlying principles. Women's clothes, say the psychologists, are governed by the Erotic or Seduction Principle. And fashion's changes, which are never entirely arbitrary, can be explained by what is called the theory of the 'Shifting Erogenous Zone'. The function of fashion is to increase the erotic appeal of the female body by constantly shifting the emphasis from one part of it to another. Hence we find that at one period the bosom is the centre of attraction; at another, the legs. And fashion never

311 See-through shirt and maxi-length coat by Yves Saint-Laurent, 1968

Examples of the
see-through dress,
which, perhaps for
obvious reasons, are
unlikely to be
universally adopted

312 See-through dress
by Rudi Gernreich,
1968.

313 See-through
dresses by Courrèges,
1968

314 See-through blouse by Rudi Gernreich, 1968

shifts its emphasis from one focus of attraction until another has been found. Thus, at the end of the 1920s, attention suddenly shifted from the legs to the back, and there have been many to prophesy that something similar would happen as the decade of the 1960s drew to its close.

So far this has not happened. The maxi-skirt has appeared, but has failed to establish itself. Instead, the short skirt of the last ten years has grown shorter and shorter. Women in the 1920s were thought very daring to expose their legs to the knee, but the young woman of today exposes the greater part of her thighs. Every year it was thought impossible for the mini-skirt to become any shorter, but shorter it *has* become. We have reached a degree of permissiveness in society which even the Twenties never attained. We are really, it would seem, at the eve of a social revolution the magnitude of which is only just beginning to be understood.

If indeed women are, this time, on the road to complete emancipation, this must have a profound effect not only on manners but on modes, for modes are but the reflection of the manners of the time. Any serious student of costume history must admit that this is true; otherwise he is driven back on the long-exploded idea that fashion's changes are purely arbitrary, or the equally untenable notion that such changes are a conspiracy of half a dozen leading designers in Paris, who, in order to sell their goods, persuade foolish women to throw away last year's dress and buy something from the new 'Spring Collection'. In the perspective of costume history it is plain that the dress of any given period is exactly suited to the social climate of the time, and indeed bears a close relation to such things as interior decoration and even architecture. It is impossible to imagine Louis XIV in the top hat and frock coat of Napoleon III; it is impossible to imagine the Empress Eugénie in the short skirts of the 1920s. Examples could be multiplied indefinitely.

Prophecy in such matters is always dangerous, even with the most profound study of social trends, but it is hard to

272

believe that the young woman of today – or tomorrow – will ever return to the hampering clothes of her great-grandmother. She is a different sort of person and lives in a different world. It may be that the extreme shortness of the mini-skirt will be modified in the comparatively near future, but it is fairly certain that the main lines of 'emancipated' costume will remain. Just as the modern young man has abandoned the superstition of gentility, so the young woman of today has rebelled against any kind of paternalism. In general, she earns enough money to clothe herself as she pleases.

Recently there has been what seems like a revival of femininity, with a definite Oriental flavour. This may point to some new development of fashion, some entirely new line, or it may be no more than a ripple on the stream, leaving its main direction undiverted and undisturbed. Only time can tell. The only certain thing, it seems, is that the desire to make oneself attractive to the opposite sex will always play a part in the clothes young people wear. Indeed, it is possible that the Seduction Principle (dressing to attract the opposite sex) may outlive the Hierarchical Principle (dressing to indicate one's position in society) and the Utility Principle (dressing for warmth and comfort). Eroticism is infinitely ingenious, and there will no doubt be many surprises in the clothes of both sexes during the years to come.

Select Bibliography

BERTIN, C. *Paris à la Mode*. London 1956.

BOEHN, MAX VON. *Modes and Manners*. 4 vols. London 1932.

BOUCHER, F. *A History of Costume in the West*. London 1967.

BRADFIELD, N. *Historical Costumes of England*. London 1938.

BRADFIELD, N. *Costume in Detail: Women's Dress 1730–1930*. London 1969.

BRADLEY, C.G. *Western World Costume*. New York 1954.

BROOKE, IRIS. *English Costume*. 6 vols. London 1931–5.

CALTHROP, D.C. *English Costume*. 4 vols. London 1946.

CUNNINGTON, C.W. *English Women's Clothing in the Nineteenth Century*. London 1937.

CUNNINGTON, C.W. *English Women's Clothing in the Present Century*. London 1952.

CUNNINGTON, C.W. and P. *Handbook of English Mediaeval Costume*. London 1952.

CUNNINGTON, C.W. and P. *Handbook of English Costume in the Sixteenth Century*. London 1954.

CUNNINGTON, C.W. and P. *Handbook of English Costume in the Seventeenth Century*. London 1955.

CUNNINGTON, C.W. and P. *Handbook of English Costume in the Eighteenth Century*. London 1957.

CUNNINGTON, C.W. and P. *Handbook of English Costume in the Nineteenth Century*. London 1959.

CUNNINGTON, C.W. and P. *A Dictionary of English Costume*. London 1960.

DAVENPORT, N. *Book of Costume*. London 1948.

DRUITT, H. *A Manual of Costume as Illustrated by Monumental Brasses*. London 1906.

EVANS, M. *Costume through the Ages*. London 1930.

FAIRHOLT, F.W. *Costume in England*. 2 vols. London 1885.

HARTLEY, D. *Medieval Costume and Life*. London 1931.

HOLLAND, V. *Hand-coloured Fashion Plates, 1770–1899*. London 1955.

HOUSTON, M.G. *Medieval Costume in England and France*. London 1939.

KELLY, F.M. and SCHWABE, R. *Historic Costume*. London 1925.

KELLY, F.M. and SCHWABE, R. *A Short History of Costume and Armour*. London 1931.

LAVER, J. *Fashion and Fashion Plates*. London 1943.

LAVER, J. *Taste and Fashion*. London 1945.

LAVER, J. *Costume*. London 1963.

LAVER, J. *Dress*. London 1966.

LESTER, K.M. *Historic Costume*. London 1942.

LELOIR, M. *Histoire du Costume*. Paris 1933.

NORRIS, H. *Costume and Fashion*. 6 vols. London 1927–33.

PLANCHÉ, V.R. *A Cyclopaedia of Costume*. 2 vols. London 1876, 1879.

VAN THIENEN, F. *The Great Age of Holland* ('Costume of the Western World'). London 1951.

WILCOX, H.T. *The Mode in Costume*. New York 1942.

List of Illustrations

Roman copy of Greek original, 50 B C–A D 50. Bronze statuette inlaid with silver. London, British Museum.

25 Head of unknown woman from Sicily. Greek, sixth century B C. Terracotta. Syracuse Museum. *Photo Soprintendenza alle Antichità, Syracuse.*

26 Head of the Muse Polyhymnia. Roman copy of Hellenistic original. Marble. Rome, Capitoline Museum. *Photo Georgina Masson.*

27 Head of Borghese Hera. Probably Roman copy of Greek original, third century B C. Marble. Copenhagen, Ny Carlsberg Glyptotek.

28 Warrior from red figure volute-krater by the Niobid Painter. Greek, perhaps Theseus, c. 470 B.C. Palermo, National Archaeological Museum. *Photo Soprintendenza alle Antichità.*

29 Warrior from red figure amphora by the Berlin Painter. Greek, early fifth century B C. London, British Museum.

30 Female dancer. Etruscan, end sixth century B C. Bronze. Boston, Museum of Fine Arts.

31 Dancers from Tomb of Leopards, Tarquinia. Etruscan, first quarter of fifth century B C. Wall-painting.

32 Vestal virgin. Roman, second century A D. Marble statue. Rome, National Museum. *Photo Mansell Collection.*

33 The Emperor Tiberius. Roman, first century A D. Marble statue. Paris, Louvre. *Photo Giraudon.*

34 'Bikini girl' from Imperial Villa, Piazza Armerina, Sicily. Roman, late third century A D. Mosaic. *Photo André Held.*

35 Drawing of Roman statues from *Monuments de Sculptures Antiques et Modernes*, Vauther and Lacour, Paris 1839.

36 Head of unknown Roman lady from pagan grave beneath St Peter's, Rome. By courtesy of Reverenda Fabbrica della Basilica di San Pietro.

37 Head from group of Three Graces. Roman. Siena, Museo dell'Opera della Cattedrale. *Photo Alinari.*

38 Head of Roman girl. Hellenistic sculpture in Egyptian style, date unknown. Rome, Capitoline Museum. *Photo Georgina Masson.*

39 Head of unknown woman. Roman, Flavian period, second century A D. Marble. Rome, Capitoline Museum.

40 Sarcophagus. Roman, late fourth century A D. Marble. Milan, S. Ambrogio Cathedral. *Photo Mansell Collection.*

41 Procession of female saints. Byzantine, set up c. 561. Mosaic. Ravenna, Church of St Apollinare Nuovo. *Photo Alinari.*

42 The Empress Theodora and her suite. Byzantine, 500–26. Mosaic. Ravenna, San Vitale. *Photo Alinari.*

43 Head of the Emperor Justinian. Byzantine, 500–26. Mosaic. Ravenna, San Vitale.

44 Head of the Empress Theodora. Byzantine, 500–26. Mosaic. Ravenna, San Vitale.

45 Four parts of Empire – Sclavinia, Germania, Gallia and Roma – paying homage to Otto III enthroned. Ottonian, 997–1000. Gospel book of Otto III. Munich, Staatsbibliothek. *Photo Hirmer Verlag.*

46 King Edward the Confessor from the Bayeux tapestry. Late eleventh century. Bayeux, Musée de la Tapisserie. *Photo Giraudon.*

47 Preparations for a wedding from *The Woman of Andros*,

Terence. MS executed at St Albans, mid twelfth century Illustration goes back through a Carolingian copy to a late classical manuscript. Oxford, Bodleian Library, MS Auct. F.2.13, f. 4v.

48 Crusader doing homage, from an English psalter. Thirteenth century. London, British Museum, MS Royal 2 A X X II, f. 220.

49 Shepherds, c. 1150, from tympanum of 'Portal of the Virgin', west porch, Chartres Cathedral. *Photo Martin Hürlimann.*

50 Sainted king and queen, c. 1150, west porch, Chartres Cathedral. *Photo Bildarchiv Marburg.*

51 The Lady Uta, founder-figure, c. 1245, west choir, Naumburg Cathedral. *Photo Helga Schmidt-Glassner.*

52 Peasant costume from the Luttrell Psalter. English, c. 1335–40. London, British Museum, MS 42130, f. 170.

53 Sir Geoffrey Luttrell with his wife and daughter-in-law, from the Luttrell Psalter. English, c. 1335–40. London, British Museum, MS 42130, f. 202v.

54 Dame Margarete de Cobham, from Cobham, Kent. English, 1375. Monumental brass rubbing. London, Victoria and Albert Museum.

55 John Coop, from Stoke Fleming, Devon. English, 1391. Monumental brass rubbing. London, by courtesy of the Society of Antiquaries. *Photo C. Bibbey.*

56 Agnes Salmon, from Arundel, Sussex. English, 1430. Monumental brass rubbing. London, Victoria and Albert Museum.

57 Robert Skern, from Kingston-upon-Thames, Surrey.

English, 1437. Monumental brass rubbing. London, Victoria and Albert Museum.

58 Probably Elizabeth Hasylden, from Little Chesterford, Essex. English, c. 1480. Monumental brass rubbing.

59 William Midwinter (d. 1501), from Northleach, Gloucestershire. English, early sixteenth century. Monumental brass rubbing.

60 *The Marriage of Giovanni (?) Arnolfini and Giovanna Cenami (?)*, 1434, Jan van Eyck. London, by courtesy of the Trustees of the National Gallery. *Photo National Gallery.*

61 Male and female costume, c. 1470. Engraving by Israel van Meckenem.

62 Male and female costume, c. 1485. Engraving by Israel van Meckenem.

63 *Wedding of Boccaccio Adimari*, c. 1470, Florentine school. Florence, Accademia. *Photo Scala.*

64 *Duchess of Urbino*, after 1473, Piero della Francesca. Florence, Uffizi.

65 *Portrait of a lady in red*, c. 1470, Florentine school. London, by courtesy of the Trustees of the National Gallery.

66 *Margaret of Denmark, Queen of Scotland* (detail), 1476, ascribed to Hugo van der Goes. Edinburgh, Holyrood Palace. Reproduced by gracious permission of Her Majesty the Queen.

67 Philip the Good, Duke of Burgundy, receiving a copy of the *Chroniques de Hainaut*. Flemish, 1448. Miniature. Brussels, Bibliothèque Royale de Belgique, MS 9242, f. 1r.

68 Christine de Pisan presenting her book of poems to Isabel of Bavaria, Queen of France. French, early fifteenth century. Miniature from *Works*

of Christine de Pisan. London, British Museum, MS Harley 4431, f. 3r.

69 Detail from *Chronique d'Angleterre*, Jean de Wavrin. Flemish, fifteenth century. London, British Museum, MS Royal 14.E.IV.

70 *Portrait of a lady*, c. 1455, Rogier van der Weyden. Washington, National Gallery of Art, Andrew Mellon Collection.

71 *Giovanna Tornabuoni*, 1488, Domenico Ghirlandaio. Lugano, Thyssen Collection. *Photo Brunel Lugano.*

72 *Nuremberg housewife and Venetian lady*, 1495, Albrecht Dürer. Drawing. Frankfurt, Stadelsches Kunstinstitut.

73 Jacob Fugger 'the Rich', the Emperor's banker, with his chief accountant Matthäus Schwarz, 1519. Miniature. Brunswick, Herzog Anton Ulrich-Museum.

74 German *Landsknecht*, c. 1530. Design for stained-glass window. London, Victoria and Albert Museum.

75 The Swiss Guards, detail from *Mass of Bolsena*, 1511–14, Raphael. Fresco. Rome, Vatican, Stanza dell'Eliodoro.

76 *Duke Henry of Saxony and his wife*, 1514, Lucas Cranach. Dresden, Gemäldegalerie.

77 *Katherine, Duchess of Saxony*, 1514, Lucas Cranach. Dresden, Gemäldegalerie.

78 *Katherina Knoblauchin*, 1532, Conrad Faber. Dublin, National Gallery of Ireland.

79 *Portrait of an unknown man*, before 1540, Bartolommeo Veneto. Rome, Galleria Nazionale. *Photo Mansell Collection.*

80 *Francis I of France*, first half of sixteenth century, attribu-

ted to François Clouet. Paris, Louvre. *Photo Garanger-Giraudon.*

81 *Helen of Bavaria*, c. 1563–6, Hans Schöpfer. Munich, Bayerische Staatsgemäldesammlungen.

82 *Jane Seymour*, c. 1536–7, Hans Holbein. Vienna, Kunsthistorisches Museum.

83 *Henry VIII*, based on original of 1537, school of Holbein. Liverpool, Walker Art Gallery.

84 Costume plate, c. 1560. Engraving by Jost Amman. London, British Museum.

85 *The Ambassadors*, 1533, Hans Holbein. London, by courtesy of the Trustees of the National Gallery.

86 *Thomas Cranmer*, 1546, Gerhardt Flicke. London, National Portrait Gallery.

87 *Emperor Charles V with his dog*, 1532, Titian. Madrid, Prado. *Photo Mas.*

88 *Anne of Austria, Queen of Spain*, 1571, Sanchez Coello. Vienna, Kunsthistorisches Museum.

89 *A tailor*, probably c. 1571, Giovanni Battista Moroni. London, by courtesy of the Trustees of the National Gallery.

90 *Portrait of a young man*, probably c. 1540, Angelo Bronzino. New York, The Metropolitan Museum of Art, H. O. Havemeyer Collection.

91 *Pierre Quthe*, 1562, François Clouet. Paris, Louvre. *Photo Giraudon.*

92 *Mary I, Queen of England*, 1554, Antonis Mor. Madrid, Prado. *Photo Mansell Collection.*

93 *Elizabeth I, 'Rainbow Portrait'*, c. 1600, style of Marcus Gheeraerts. Reproduced by

permission of the Marquess of Salisbury KG, Hatfield House. *Photo Courtauld Institute of Art.*

94 *Magdalena, Duchess of Neuburg, c.* 1613, formerly attributed to Peter Candid (de Witte). Munich, Alte Pinakothek. *Photo Joachim Blauel.*

95 *Queen Elizabeth at Blackfriars, c.* 1600, Marcus Gheeraerts. Collection Simon Wingfield Digby MP, Sherborne Castle. *Photo Fleming.*

96 Elizabeth, Briget and Susan, 1589, from tomb of their grandmother Mildred, Lady Burghley. London, Westminster Abbey. Crown copyright. *Photo Royal Commission on Historical Monuments.*

97 Sir Robert Burghley, 1589, from tomb of his mother Mildred, Lady Burghley. London, Westminster Abbey. Crown copyright. *Photo Royal Commission on Historical Monuments.*

98 Elizabethan costume, from *Description of England.* Anonymous drawing. Flemish, late sixteenth century. London, British Museum, MS Add. 28330.

99 *Rubens and his wife Isabella Brant,* 1610, Peter Paul Rubens. Munich, Alte Pinakothek.

100 *Sigmund Feierabendt, the bibliophile,* 1587. Engraving by J. Sadeler.

101 *Ball given at the Court of Henry III in honour of the marriage of the Duc de Joyeuse,* late sixteenth century, French school. Paris, Louvre. *Photo Giraudon.*

102 *Sir Christopher Hatton,* 1589, Anonymous. London, National Portrait Gallery.

103 *Sir Walter Raleigh, c.* 1588, Anonymous. London, National Portrait Gallery.

104 *Richard Sackville, Earl of Dorset,* 1616, Isaac Oliver. Miniature. London, Victoria and Albert Museum.

105 French nobleman, 1629. Etching by Abraham Bosse.

106 French nobleman, *c.* 1630. Etching by Abraham Bosse.

107 French nobleman, *c.* 1636. Etching by Abraham Bosse.

108 French noblewoman, *c.* 1636. Etching by Abraham Bosse.

109 *Gallery of the Palais Royal, c.* 1640. Engraving by Abraham Bosse. Paris, Musée Carnavalet. *Photo Giraudon.*

110 *Henry Rich, 1st Earl of Holland,* 1640, studio of Daniel Mytens. London, National Portrait Gallery.

111 *Wedding celebration,* 1637, Wolfgang Heimbach. Bremen, Kunsthalle.

112 *Autumn, c.* 1650. Engraved by R. Gaywood after W. Hollar.

113 *Portrait of a middle-aged woman with hands folded,* 1633, Frans Hals. London, by courtesy of the Trustees of the National Gallery.

114 Suit with petticoat breeches, *c.* 1665. Edinburgh, Royal Scottish Museum. *Photo Tom Scott.*

115 *Two ladies of the Lake Family, c.* 1660, Peter Lely. London, by courtesy of the Trustees of the Tate Gallery.

116 Sir Thomas Isham's wedding suit, *c.* 1681. London, Victoria and Albert Museum.

117 *Charles II on horseback, c.* 1670. Engraving by Pieter Stevensz.

118 *Sir Robert Shirley,* 1622, Anthony van Dyck. Courtesy the Treasury, The National Trust (Lord Egremont Collection, Petworth).

119 *Duke of Burgundy, c.* 1695. Engraving by R. Bonnart.

120 *Homme de qualité jouant de la basse de viole,* 1695. Engraving by J.D. de Saint-Jean.

121 *Dame de la plus haute qualité,* 1693. Engraving by J.D. de Saint-Jean.

122 *Femme de qualité en déshabille d'étoffe siamoise,* 1687, Engraving by J.D. de Saint-Jean.

123 *Mode bourgeoise, c.* 1690, from *Costume Époque Louis XIV,* vol. I. Engraving by N. Guerard. New York, The J. Pierpoint Morgan Library.

124–7 Four French costumes, end seventeenth century. Engravings by S. le Clerc.

128 *James Stuart and his sister Louisa Maria Theresa,* 1695, Nicolas de Largillière. London, National Portrait Gallery.

129 Wedding procession, 1674, from *Relazione del regno di Svezia,* Lorenzo Magalotti. Drawing. Stockholm, Nordiska Museet.

130 *Madame de Pompadour,* 1759, François Boucher. London, reproduced by permission of the Trustees of the Wallace Collection.

131 *Martin Folkes, c.* 1740. Mezzotint by James McArdell after Thomas Hudson.

132 *Lord Mohun, c.* 1710, Godfrey Kneller. London, National Portrait Gallery.

133 *The five orders of periwigs,* 1761. Engraving by William Hogarth.

134 *Lady Howard, c.* 1710. Mezzotint by J. Smith after Godfrey Kneller.

135 *Mrs Anastasia Robinson, c.* 1723. Mezzotint by J. Faber after Vanderbank.

136 Sketches of three figures, Antoine Watteau (1684–1721). Chalk drawing. Berlin, Kupferstichkabinett.

193 Day dresses, 1853. Fashion plate from *Le Follet*.

194 *A Windy Corner*, 1864. Anonymous lithograph. London, Victoria and Albert Museum.

195 Girls in crinoline dresses and pantaloons, 1853. From *Die Tafel Birnen*.

196 Crinoline petticoat, *c.* 1860. Fashion plate.

197 Paris fashions for September 1859. Fashion plate from *Illustrated London News*.

198 *In a box at the Opera*, 1857. Fashion plate from *Le Follet*.

199 Mrs Amelia Bloomer, *c.* 1850. Anonymous engraving.

200 *Une tournure à faire tourner toutes les têtes!*, 1858. Lithograph by Charles Vernier. London, Victoria and Albert Museum.

201 *The Empress Eugénie and her maids of honour*, *c.* 1860, Francis Xavier Winterhalter. Compiègne Chateau. *Photo Giraudon*.

202 Crinoline dress, *c.* 1860, by Worth. Drawing on lithograph model. London, Victoria and Albert Museum.

203 London and Paris fashions for June 1864. Fashion plate.

204 *Women in the garden*, 1866–7, Claude Monet. Paris, Louvre. *Photo Giraudon*.

205 London and Paris fashions for March 1869. Fashion plate.

206 Headdresses, August 1870. Fashion plate from *Le Journal des Modes*.

207 Duke of Edinburgh and Grand Duchess Marie Alexandrovna, *c.* 1870. Fashion plate from *Tailor and Cutter*.

208 Lady's and child's dresses, September 1873. Fashion plate from *Journal des Demoiselles*.

209 *Madame Moitessier*, 1844/5–56, J.-A.-D. Ingres. London, by courtesy of the Trustees of the National Gallery. *Photo National Gallery*.

210 *Derby Day*, 1856–8, William Powell Frith. London, by courtesy of the Trustees of the Tate Gallery.

211 *Omnibus Life in London*, 1859, William Egley. London, by courtesy of the Trustees of the Tate Gallery.

212 Ladies' and child's costume, March 1877. Fashion plate from *Journal des Demoiselles*.

213 Evening dresses, *c.* 1877. Fashion plate from *Le Follet*.

214 *Too Early*, 1873, James Jacques Tissot. London, Guildhall Art Gallery.

215 *La Grande Jatte*, 1884–6, Georges Seurat. Chicago, Art Institute, Helen Birch Bartlett Memorial Collection.

216 Evening and visiting dress, 1884. Fashion plate from *Le Moniteur de la Mode*.

217 *Nincompoopiana – The Mutual Admiration Society*, 1880, George du Maurier. From *Punch*, February 1880.

218 'Langtry' and other bustles, 1870s–80s. Advertisements.

219 *The Reception*, 1886, James Jacques Tissot. New York, Albright-Knox Art Gallery, Buffalo. Bequest of Mr William Chase.

220 *The Picnic*, 1875, James Jacques Tissot. London, by courtesy of the Trustees of the Tate Gallery. *Photo Tate Gallery*.

221 *Les Parapluies*, *c.* 1884, Pierre-Auguste Renoir. London, by courtesy of the Trustees of the National Gallery.

222 Male and female cycling costume of 1878–80. Fashion plates.

223 Male and female seaside costume, 1886. Fashion plate from *The West End Gazette*.

224 Male and female costume, 1884. Fashion plate from *British Costume for Spring and Summer*.

225 *Count Robert de Montesquiou*, 1897, Giovanni Boldini. Paris, Musée National de l'art moderne. *Photo Giraudon*.

226 Knickerbocker cycling costume for ladies, 1894. *Der Bazar*, Berlin.

227 Walking dresses, 1891. Fashion plate from *Der Bazar*, Berlin.

228 Female riding costume, February 1894. Fashion plate from *The West End Gazette*.

229 Autumn walking dress, 1895. Fashion plate from *Wiener Mode*, Vienna.

230 Dress at the races, 1894. Fashion plate from *Le Salon de la Mode*, Paris.

231 Travelling costume, 1898. Fashion plate.

232 Walking dress, February 1899. Fashion plate.

233 *The Wertheimer Sisters*, *c.* 1901, John Singer Sargent. London, by courtesy of the Trustees of the Tate Gallery.

234 *Il a été primé*, evening dress, 1914. Fashion plate from *La Gazette du Bon Ton*.

235 *Madame Jasmy Alvin*, 1928, Kees van Dongen. Paris, Musée National de l'art moderne. *Photo Giraudon*.

236 Spring dress trimmed with silk braid, May 1900. Fashion plate from *Illustrated London News*.

237 Spring dress trimmed with lace, May 1900. Fashion plate from *Illustrated London News*.

238 Straight-fronted corset, February 1902. Advertisement.

239 Chiffon dress, 1901. Fashion plate.

240 Evening dress, September 1901. Fashion plate.

241 Summer dress, c. 1903. Manchester, Museum of Costume, Platt Hall.

242 Silk evening dress, 1911. Manchester, Museum of Costume, Platt Hall.

243 Evening dress, 1907–8. Manchester, Museum of Costume, Platt Hall.

244 'Merveilleuse' dresses, May 1908.

245 Dress, 1908.

246 Lady's golfing costume, 1907. Fashion plate from *Ladies' Tailor*.

247 Day dress, 1907. Fashion plate from *Ladies' Tailor*.

248 Male summer costume, July 1907. Fashion plate from *London Fashion Review*.

249 Walking dress, 1910. Fashion plate from *Ladies' Tailor*.

250 Lady's motoring costume, April 1905. *Photo Radio Times Hulton Picture Library*.

251 Male flannel suit for boating, July 1902. *Photo Radio Times Hulton Picture Library*.

252 Male motoring costume, c. 1904. Fashion plate from *Tailor and Cutter*. *Photo Radio Times Hulton Picture Library*.

253 Hobble-skirt dresses, 1910. From *The Sketch*, 25 May 1910.

254 Hobble garter, 1910. From *The Sketch*, 2 November 1910.

255 Male and female dress at the races, 1914. *Photo Ullstein, Berlin*.

256 Hobble-skirt dress at Auteuil races, 1914. *Photo Radio Times Hulton Picture Library*.

257 Dress, 1913. Fashion plate from *Journal des Dames et des Modes*.

258 'Robe Sorbet' by Paul Poiret, 1911. *Photo Collection de l'Union Française des Arts du Costume, Paris*.

259 Dress by Paul Poiret, 1913. *Photo Collection de l'Union Française des Arts du Costume, Paris*.

260 Dress by Paul Poiret, 1913. *Photo Collection de l'Union Française des Arts du Costume, Paris*.

261 Day dress, 1912. Fashion plate from *Journal des Dames et des Modes*.

262 Evening dress by Paquin, 1913. Fashion plate from *Gazette du Bon Ton*.

263 Day dress, 1914. Fashion plate from *Journal des Dames et des Modes*.

264 Wartime coat and skirt, 1916. London, Victoria and Albert Museum.

265 Summer dress, 1915. London, Victoria and Albert Museum.

266 Day dresses, June 1919. Fashion plate from *Vogue*, Late June 1919. *Photo by courtesy of* Vogue *magazine*.

267 Evening dresses, 1919. Fashion plate from *Moderne Welt*, Vienna.

268 Day dresses and velvet dress, 1921. Fashion plate from *Chiffons*.

269 Foulard silk summer dress, 1920. *Photo Ullstein, Berlin*.

270 Summer dresses, 1926. Fashion plate from *Les Idées Nouvelles*.

271 Ladies at the Ritz, London, 1926. Fashion plate from *Vogue*, Early April 1926. *Photo by courtesy of* Vogue *magazine*.

272 Lady's tweed suit, 1929. Fashion plate from *Ladies' Tailor Fashions*.

273 Lady's corset, 1924. From *Vogue*, Early February 1924. *Photo by courtesy of* Vogue *magazine*.

274 Dresses by Chanel, 1926. Fashion plate from *Vogue*, Late April 1926. *Photo by courtesy of* Vogue *magazine*.

275 At Chester races, 1926. *Photo Ullstein, Berlin*.

276 Afternoon coat, 1928. *Photo Ullstein, Berlin*.

277 At Longchamps races, 1930. *Photo Ullstein, Berlin*.

278 'Pierrette' hair-style by Jeanne Lanvin, 1928. Sketch from Jeanne Lanvin Collections, Paris.

279 Evening dress, 1929. Fashion plate from *Vogue*, 15 May 1929. *Photo by courtesy of* Vogue *magazine*.

280 Day dress by Jeanne Lanvin, summer 1931. Sketch from Jeanne Lanvin Collections, Paris.

281 Evening dress by Jeanne Lanvin, 1931. Sketch from Jeanne Lanvin Collections, Paris.

282 Evening dress by Worth, 1930.

283 Evening dress, 1932. Fashion drawing by Jean Maillart. London, Victoria and Albert Museum.

284 Dresses at Berlin races, 1930. *Photo Ullstein, Berlin*.

285 Suit, 1935. *Photo Radio Times Hulton Picture Library*.

286 Dresses for the races, May 1935. Fashion plate.

287 Summer dress, 1934. *Photo Ullstein, Berlin*.

288 'Butterfly' sleeve dress, 1934. *Photo Ullstein, Berlin*.

289 'Butterfly' sleeve dress from Vienna, 1934. *Photo Ullstein, Berlin*.

290 Fashion shows in a salon, 1935. *Photo Ullstein, Berlin*.

291 Dresses at the races, 1938. *Photo Ullstein, Berlin*.

292 Paris fashions, June 1939. Fashion plate from *Vogue*, 14 June 1939. *Photo by courtesy of* Vogue *magazine*.

Index

Italic figures refer to pages on which illustrations appear